Edwin Cannan

Elementary Political Economy

Edwin Cannan

Elementary Political Economy

ISBN/EAN: 9783744645584

Printed in Europe, USA, Canada, Australia, Japan

Cover: Foto ©Suzi / pixelio.de

More available books at **www.hansebooks.com**

Elementary

Political Economy

BY

EDWIN CANNAN, M.A.

BALLIOL COLLEGE

London

HENRY FROWDE

OXFORD UNIVERSITY PRESS WAREHOUSE

AMEN CORNER

1888

[All rights reserved]

CONTENTS.

SECT.   PAGE

INTRODUCTION 1

PART I: GENERAL MATERIAL WELFARE.

1. Labour 3
2. Useful material objects 6
3. The productiveness of industry 11
4. The productiveness of industry increased by the growth of knowledge 12
5. The productiveness of industry increased by the accumulation of useful material objects 14
6. The productiveness of industry increased by the growth of co-operation between individuals 16
7. The productiveness of industry as affected by variations in population 21

PART II: INDIVIDUAL WELFARE UNDER PRIVATE PROPERTY.

1. Complexity introduced by exchange 26
2. Kinds of things which can be exchanged 28
3. A medium of exchange 30
4. Characteristics of a good medium of exchange . . . 32
5. Credit: undertakings to pay the medium of exchange given instead of the medium itself 35
6. Sources of individuals' incomes 39
7. Why property is a source of income 39
8. Different ways of deriving income from labour . . . 44
9. Different ways of deriving income from property . . 56
10. The comparative size of individuals' incomes dependent on values 64

CONTENTS.

SECT.		PAGE
11.	The value of a commodity	66
12.	The comparison or measurement of the values of commodities	69
13.	Causes on which the comparative values of commodities depend	72
14.	The comparison of incomes	79
15.	Causes which determine the comparative size of the incomes individuals derive from labour	82
16.	Causes which determine the comparative size of the incomes individuals derive from property	99
17.	Causes which determine the comparative size of the income derived from property and the income derived from labour	102

PART III: THE PROMOTION OF PUBLIC WELFARE BY THE STATE.

1.	Character of the co-operation involved in State effort after wealth	116
2.	Protection	121
3.	The sale of commodities by the State	129
4.	The gratuitous provision of benefits by the State . .	133
5.	Contributions to the State	138

INTRODUCTION.

The aim of Political Economy is the explanation of the general causes on which the wealth or material welfare of human beings depends.

To explain why such and such a nation or class is rich, and such and such other nation or class is poor, is the duty of the historian, just as to explain why such and such an individual was rich or poor is the duty of the biographer. The duty of the political economist is, so far as possible, to explain generally what has made and will make mankind and nations wealthy, and also, given certain institutions and states of human nature, what has made and will make individuals wealthy. With regard to the wealth of mankind and of nations the generalisations of political economy are universally true; they are independent of changes of human character and institutions. But with regard to the wealth of individuals the case is different. There are no laws regarding the determination of the wealth of individuals which are universally true. The causes which make individuals rich and poor vary with the customs and institutions which are established. The economist may attempt to explain the causes which determine the material welfare of individuals under any existing institutions and customs, or he may attempt to explain the causes which determined the material welfare of individuals under institutions or customs which have existed, or he may take the much more dangerous course of attempting to explain what would determine the material welfare of individuals under wholly imaginary institutions and customs. The most usual and the most profitable course is for the economist to take as a basis the institutions and customs which exist in his own country and in his own time.

In the first part of this work the attempt is made to explain the general causes on which the material welfare of mankind and of nations always depends. The second part deals with the causes which at present in this country, and in other countries which resemble it, determine the material welfare of individuals if we exclude as far as possible the effects of State action. The third part shows how the results of these causes are modified by the more ordinary actions of the State in a country like our own.

PART I.

GENERAL MATERIAL WELFARE.

§ 1. Labour.

That mankind as a whole can attain wealth only by means of human labour is a truth which needs no demonstration. Under some conditions individuals can attain wealth without themselves personally labouring, but they can never attain it without some human being having laboured. The amount of labour necessary to attain a certain amount of wealth is different at different times and places. Sometimes it is very great and sometimes very small, but it can never be diminished down to nothing. Without labour mankind would necessarily perish off the face of the globe, even if all soils were fertile and all climates temperate.

It is a much more common mistake to over-estimate the good of labour than to under-estimate it. We so often hear of people 'asking for work' and complaining of 'want of work' or of the absence of 'demand for labour,' that most of us are tempted at some time or other to look on labour as something desirable in itself, of which there is not enough for every one. Whole nations have often acted, through their governments, as if this were really the case. For fear that they might not have enough work to do, they have enacted laws which make the attainment of wealth more laborious; they have directed their efforts not towards the increase of wealth but towards the increase of the labour requisite to attain wealth. Similarly, a writer once maintained that the Great Fire of London was a most fortunate occurrence, because it gave so much work to do in rebuilding; so too, many people regard with a certain amount of disfavour the introduction of machinery, on the ground that it does so much work so quickly that it 'takes away employment'—does not leave enough work for human hands to do.

Yet it is quite clear to anyone who can take a comprehensive view of all industry, that there can be no such thing as a general want of work; the possibility of working is unlimited. Under our present social arrangements men are often 'out of work,' but this is not because there is too little work altogether to be done, but because, owing to various circumstances, certain people offer to do what is little or not at all required instead of what is much required. If, for instance, more ships are very little wanted, and many thousand persons offer to work at the building of additional ships, very likely many of them will be 'out of work,' but it does not follow that they would be out of work if they were able and willing to produce something which is more required than ships. Before there can be 'a general scarcity of work' the world must be completely supplied not only with ships, but with everything it desires to have; and this is obviously impossible. At present the world is very insufficiently supplied even with food, clothes, and houses, and the average income of each human being is a most beggarly pittance even in the wealthiest countries; the whole industry of the world is evidently as yet quite inadequate to keep everyone in the most meagre degree of comfort. Even if everyone had three good meals a day and two suits of clothes a year and two rooms, would there be nothing more left for labour to supply? Should we not want more furniture, more books, more gardens, more of all sorts of things which can only be produced by labour? Clearly the number of workers can never be 'in excess of the work to be done,' for the work to be done is infinite.

Even if there were any chance of 'the work to be done' coming to an end, that would not appear a very terrible prospect to most people. Everywhere around we see people labouring, some of them morning, noon, and night, but we know very well that they do not do so, as a rule, because they like it, but because they like certain good things which they cannot otherwise obtain. No doubt a skilful painter may find the painting of a picture an agreeable work apart from the good things he may expect to get by selling it, but the pleasure does not consist in the actual labour or drudgery, but in the pride of skill which fills his mind as he sees the picture being created by his hand; in the labour without the picture there could be no pleasure. In the majority of cases it is still more evident that labour is not desirable for its own sake. Most people labour not 'for the pleasure of working,' as some artists, authors, and others are said to do, but for food, lodging, and other necessaries of life, and they readily admit that the less work they have to do in order to obtain a given amount of those satisfactions the better they are pleased. Possibly the mass of mankind is wrong in considering the necessity of labour as a curse rather than a blessing. Wrong or right however, its opinion is shared by most of those who are afraid of general 'over-production' and a 'universal want of work'; they do not love labour for its own sake any more than others do. 'A universal want of work,' accompanied by the production of too many good things (whatever too many good things may be), ought then to present no terrors to them.

Every nation, as well as every individual, should endeavour to attain wealth with as little labour as possible.

§ 2. Useful Material Objects.

The immediate aim of many kinds of labour is that which is called by economists the 'production,' and by ordinary people the 'making,' of useful material objects. Man cannot, of course, create matter, so that the production or making of useful material objects only consists in so shaping or placing matter that it may be useful. The corn-grower places seed in the ground, which he has moved in such a way that earth, seed, and atmosphere turn into the useful object called a crop; then he separates the crop from the ground and the grain from the chaff; then the miller places the grain between revolving stones and 'produces' flour; lastly the baker places the flour with other ingredients in a hot oven and 'produces' bread.

Now when the process of making a useful material object is finished, that object does not pass beyond the ken of the economist; it is not done with. To be useful, a material object must be used. It must be used either in the production of another useful material object, as flour and ovens are used in the production of bread, or in the production of some pleasure or the prevention of some pain, as bread is used in the production of the pleasure of eating or in the prevention of the pain of hunger. If it is used in the production of another useful material object, it is indirectly useful; if it is used in the production of a pleasure or prevention of a pain, it is directly useful. To suppose that material objects can be desirable for their own sakes is a gross error. They can only be desirable as the means or instruments which must necessarily be used before certain pleasures can be obtained or pains averted. Starvation can only be averted by using the material objects which constitute food, and therefore those material objects are desirable;

but what we work for and want is not the food itself but the prevention of starvation. If hunger could be appeased by murmuring a short incantation, we should desist from cultivating the soil. So too the comfort of being warm and dry can only be obtained by using the material object called a house, and therefore houses are desirable; but what we work for is not a house but the comfort of being sheltered from the elements; the worse the climate the more elaborate the house. If neither rain nor dew ever fell, if no wind ever blew, if it was never too hot and never too cold, and if there were no murderers, robbers, wild animals, snakes and insects, we should probably not trouble ourselves with building houses at all.

Economists have sometimes written as if mankind existed simply to increase the number of material objects in certain shapes and forms which are on the earth at any particular moment. They have treated men as machines to be used and worn out in keeping up and increasing a sacred mass of matter. The truth is, however, that useful material objects are only brought into existence in order to be instrumental in making human life enjoyable. Much necessary and important labour is expended not in the production of useful material objects but in causing pleasure or preventing pain directly. The physician and the musician, for instance, can scarcely be said to produce useful material objects. The ultimate aim of the labour which produces useful material objects is the same as the aim of the labour which produces no material objects—that is to say, it is the promotion of human comfort and happiness. A nation is well or ill off according as this aim is well or ill attained, not according as it produces or has collected a large or small number of instruments for the attainment of that aim.

While no useful material object is more than an instrument for the attainment of some satisfaction, no such object is less than an instrument for that purpose. All useful material objects without exception are 'instruments of production.' The air, the sea, and the land, are instruments of production just as much as ploughs and steam-engines; the air we all use in the production of health, the sea is an instrument of production similar to a road or a railway, the land is used in the production of everything.

It is useless to attempt to divide any actual stock of useful material objects into objects used in the production of other useful material objects on the one hand, and objects used in the production of comfort directly on the other hand. Many, we might almost say most, useful material objects are used both in the production of other such objects and in the direct production of satisfactions. For instance, most of the instruments used in conveying goods from place to place are also used in conveying persons from place to place, and are therefore used both in the direct and indirect production of satisfactions. So too a meadow is often used both to feed a cow and to please the owner's eye, and buildings are constantly used to keep both men and materials dry. Even if the division in question could be satisfactorily made, it does not seem that anything would be gained by making it: whether a thing is useful for the purpose of producing enjoyment directly, or for the purpose of producing some other thing which will be useful for that purpose, is surely a matter of very little importance.

It is equally vain to attempt to divide useful material objects into natural objects (called shortly 'Land') on the one hand, and objects produced by labour on the other. Land itself, so soon as it is cultivated, ceases to be a natural object: but cultivated land can scarcely be said to be an object produced by labour; some of its properties are due to nature and some to labour. Nor is land proper the only natural object which can be improved by labour and thus cease to be strictly a natural object. A river ceases to be a natural object as soon as its bed is improved by dredging. Except the air and the open sea it would be difficult to find any useful material object which is wholly unimproved by labour.

Useful material objects vary as to their perishability. Some of them, such as the ocean and diamonds, do not 'decay of themselves,' and are not worn out by use. Some of them, such as bridges and pictures, are not worn out by use, but decay of themselves—that is to say, in consequence of the action of the natural forces to which they are necessarily exposed. Some of them, such as clothes and steam-boilers, are worn out by use. Some of them both decay of themselves and are worn out by use; among these are most kinds of buildings. Animals and vegetables die, and food and fuel are 'used up' or 'consumed.' The things which die we may class with those which decay of themselves, and the things which are used up or consumed we may class with those which are worn out by use.

§ 3. The Productiveness of Industry.

At one time it seems to have almost been thought that a nation was well or ill off according as the aggregate amount of comfort obtained was great or small. A country with a population of forty millions would have been considered richer than a country with a population of twenty millions, if the forty millions taken all together enjoyed more comforts than the twenty millions taken all together. Nowadays we should say, much more reasonably, that the richer country of the two would be that in which the average comfort per head, not the aggregate comfort, was greatest.

Given a certain amount of labour, the average comfort of a collection of individuals per head will depend on the quantity of comfort a given amount of labour will produce. When this is a great quantity we say that 'the productiveness of industry' is great, and when it is small we say that 'the productiveness of industry' is small.

As the world has grown older the productiveness of industry has, in spite of possible temporary or local diminutions, pretty steadily increased. No one, however pessimistic, really doubts that the population of the earth as a whole can now produce more comforts or pleasures per head by an hour's labour than it could a thousand years ago. In the more civilised countries of the world the difference is very striking; scarcely anywhere is it altogether imperceptible. The ultimate causes of this increase of the productiveness of industry are, we may reasonably suppose, the same as the ultimate causes of all human progress; what these are it is not our business here to try to discover. We must be content with the immediate causes, which appear to be three in number.

§ 4. The Productiveness of Industry increased by the Growth of Knowledge.

The first, and perhaps the most important, of the three causes which have led to the increase of the productiveness of industry is increase of knowledge. As regards this cause it is scarcely necessary to say anything. Everyone can see how enormously the productiveness of industry has been increased by the growth of men's knowledge of mechanics, chemistry, electricity, and other departments of science. In consequence of the growth of knowledge a few men can now do not only what it used to require many men to do, but also what could not formerly have been done by any number of men in any length of time. A hundred years ago in this country very probably a certain amount of labour could produce as much and as good cloth as a considerably less amount of labour can produce at present, but it is certain that no amount of labour whatever could then convey a person from London to Grantham in two hours. Nor must we suppose, as we are sometimes inclined to do, that all important inventions and discoveries have been made in modern times. The inventions of modern times are certainly not of greater importance than those which took place in a remote antiquity; beside fire, the alphabet, the wheel, and the cultivation of cereals, our modern discoveries do not appear quite so marvellous as we generally consider them.

In every art small improvements are constantly being suggested by the teaching of experience, so that the productiveness of industry is being slowly but surely increased by the increase of knowledge, even when there is an absence of the more brilliant inventions and discoveries. So long as experience continues to teach, there is no fear of the human race reaching what used to be the bugbear of some economists, 'a stationary state.'

§ 5. The Productiveness of Industry increased by the accumulation of Useful Material Objects.

The second of the three causes which have led to the increase of the productiveness of industry is the increase which has taken place in the quantity of the useful material objects which have been accumulated or saved. It is not perhaps very clear how the world's stock of useful material objects ought to be measured, but its increase is usually apparent enough: when we see almost all kinds of useful material objects being added to everywhere, and very few disappearing or falling into decay without being replaced, we can say pretty safely that the whole stock is increasing, even if we do not know exactly how much of one sort of useful material object is equal to a given quantity of another sort. That in long periods of time the stock has increased not only absolutely, but also in proportion to the population, we can have no manner of doubt.

As to the effects of the increase of the stock of useful material objects on the productiveness of industry, on the amount of comfort or enjoyment which can be obtained by a given amount of labour, we have only to imagine what would be our condition if every trace of past labour were magically effaced from this country. We should be left on a thickly wooded and swampy island, naked, surrounded by wild beasts, shelterless, and with nothing ready to eat. Assiduous labour for hours might possibly enable some of us to knock down a rabbit with a pebble or stick, and if we were not lucky enough to be able to light a fire by friction we should be glad to eat it raw.

The method by which mankind increases its stock of useful material objects is more often misunderstood than the effects of an increase of the stock. As we have already observed, many useful material objects are from different reasons perishable. In consequence of this fact, a large portion of the labour of mankind has always to be expended in executing what would in a private business be called 'renewals and repairs'; the useful material objects which perish in parts rather than altogether have to be mended or repaired, and those which perish altogether have to be replaced or renewed. Another large portion of the labour of mankind is expended in the production of satisfactions directly, and not in the production (including of course in that term the repair and renewal) of useful material objects. Now if the whole of the labour spent in producing useful material objects is, owing to whatever cause, less than what is sufficient to maintain the stock of those objects, that stock must obviously deteriorate or decrease; if, on the other hand, the whole of the labour spent in producing useful material objects is more than what is sufficient to maintain the stock of those objects, that stock must as obviously improve or increase. If the world, for instance, wishes to add to its stock of useful material objects a waterway through some isthmus, all that is necessary is that it should construct the canal, while at the same time maintaining its already existing stock by the necessary repairs and renewals. To do this would of course be physically impossible if the productiveness of industry were so small that the whole labour of the world had to be expended in merely keeping people alive. In order that the canal may be made, it is necessary that the men who are constructing it should be maintained (that is, daily provided with all that they use up or wear out) by the rest of the workers of the world, who must at the same time provide for themselves.

The process of adding to the stock of useful material objects is called 'saving,' a word which combines the meaning of 'storing up,' and 'sparing' or abstaining from some enjoyment. The addition to the stock is what is stored up, and the enjoyment which might have been immediately obtained by the labour which was actually expended in making the addition to the stock is what is abstained from.

§ 6. THE PRODUCTIVENESS OF INDUSTRY INCREASED BY THE GROWTH OF CO-OPERATION BETWEEN INDIVIDUALS.

The third cause of the increase which has taken place in the productiveness of industry is the growth of co-operation between individuals. At one time the circles within which individuals co-operated or worked together were small—for most purposes not larger than the family or village community. The tendency of civilisation has been to enlarge the area of co-operation, till now we see the production of many good things carried on by innumerable individuals working together all over the globe. Even in Adam Smith's time it was possible for him to say:—'Observe the accommodation of the most common artificer or day-labourer in a civilised and thriving country, and you will perceive that the number of people of whose industry a part, though but a small part, has been employed in procuring him this accommodation exceeds all computation. The woollen coat, for example, which covers the day labourer, as coarse and rough as it may appear, is the produce of the joint labour of a great multitude of workmen. The shepherd, the sorter of the wool, the woolcomber or carder, the dyer, the scribbler, the spinner, the weaver, the fuller, the dresser, with many others, must all join their different arts in order to complete even this homely production.' Since Adam Smith wrote, co-operation between individuals generally, and especially co-operation between individuals living far apart, has continued to increase.

The chief reasons why co-operation between individuals assists the productiveness of industry are four. The first and most obvious is that co-operation enables some things to be done which the physical strength of any single individual is incapable of doing. We often hear astonishment expressed at the force which machinery places at men's command; but it must not be forgotten that the labour of many men is usually necessary to make a machine, and that even when the machine is made, though one man may guide it, more than one man is usually required to work it. When all is prepared, one man may be able to start a huge steam-ship, but the co-operation of many men will be required to keep it going. It is clear that if individuals had to live in isolation, without receiving any assistance from each other, no great work could be undertaken. The second reason why co-operation increases the productiveness of industry is that it allows labour or employments to be divided or distributed among individuals in such a way that each kind of labour is done by specialists, by people who have become by study or practice particularly well able to do that kind of labour. 'A Jack of all trades' is proverbially ' master of none.' It is certain that no man could have the training and experience necessary to enable him to do all the work now done for him by carpenters, blacksmiths, bookbinders, fishermen, and tailors, as easily and well as they do it. Still less could any man be at once a good surgeon, astronomer, artist, watchmaker, navvy, and accountant. The third reason why co-operation increases the productiveness of industry is that it enables each kind of work to be done by those who are best fitted by nature to do it. When co-operation prevails, he who has bodily strength but not much mind may be put to work which requires strength and no great degree of intelligence, and he who has much mind but not much bodily strength may be put to work which requires intelligence and not much strength. In this respect we are at present very far from having obtained all possible advantage from co-operation; we much too often see the wrong man in the wrong place. Still, we see men, women, and children doing on the whole the kinds of work for which those three classes of human beings are respectively best naturally fitted. The fourth reason why co-operation increases the productiveness of industry is that it enables many kinds of work to be done in the places where it is easiest to do them. The advantage of carrying on different kinds of work so far as possible in the places best fitted for them, has never perhaps had its existence explicitly denied, but it is often ignored by the supporters of a certain fiscal policy. In agriculture the advantage of producing one thing in one place and another in another place is very apparent. One climate and soil suit one crop, and another climate and soil suit another crop or series of crops; anyone can see that the productiveness of industry would not be so great as it is if the inhabitants of each square mile of the earth's surface were obliged to grow on that particular square mile the whole of the food they require—corn, cattle, sheep, vegetables, tea, sugar, and everything else. As to minerals, it is evident that it is only possible to get them from particular places. In manufactures the advantage arising from 'the localisation of industry,' as it is called, is not quite so apparent, but consideration shows it to exist. It is easier to manufacture iron goods where the iron ore and coal lie close together, than to carry the ironstone or the coal to a distance and then do the work, and many manufacturing operations can only be easily carried on in particular climates. It needs no demonstration to show that the localisation of industry, or carrying on of each kind of work in the place best fitted for it, can only exist in consequence of co-operation. Without co-operation each man must do all kinds of work, and all kinds of work must consequently be done in each place where men happen to be settled.

There is one drawback the existence of which prevents the progress of co-operation from increasing the productiveness of industry quite so much as might be expected. This is the impossibility of securing that the whole labour of the population of the world should be expended in producing always exactly the things which are most wanted. An isolated man co-operating with nobody would, of course, easily manage to divide his time between the different kinds of labour in such a way as to make his labour as productive as possible: if more thirsty than hungry he would not spend his time looking for food till he had looked for water. But when employments are divided among a great number of individuals, and industries are localised, it is not so easy to distribute the whole of the labour so as to make it as productive as possible. It may very well happen that, owing to some passing cause, too many people are doing one kind of work and too few people are doing some other kind. The quantity of each kind of work done comes to depend on the numbers of people employed in each kind of work; and it is not easy to take a man away from the kind of work to which he is accustomed and set him to another kind of work, even when it is discovered that too much of the one kind of work and too little of the other is being done. Moreover, that discovery often does not take place till much injury has been done to the productiveness of industry.

It may be observed in conclusion that to be of much service co-operation must be willing co-operation. The unwilling co-operation of the slave with his master and his fellow slaves is perhaps more favourable to the productiveness of industry than no co-operation at all, but it is not so favourable as willing co-operation. A man will not, in most kinds of industry, produce as much in an hour when he is unwilling as he will produce when he is willing, and yet he may have laboured just as hard—may be just as tired; the unwilling labour is less productive than the willing labour.

§ 7. THE PRODUCTIVENESS OF INDUSTRY AS AFFECTED BY VARIATIONS IN POPULATION.

Under certain circumstances the productiveness of industry in a country or countries may be affected by an increase or decrease of the population of the country or countries in question. It is not true that an increase of population must always diminish the productiveness of industry, or that a decrease of population must always increase the productiveness of industry. No more is it true that an increase of population must always increase the productiveness of industry, or that a decrease of population must always diminish it. The truth is that the productiveness of industry is sometimes promoted by an increase of population, and sometimes by a decrease of population.

The only real 'Law of Population' is simply this:—At any given time the amount of labour which can be exerted on a given extent of land, consistently with the attainment of the greatest productiveness of industry possible at that time, is definite. Assuming (what within short periods is almost exactly true) that the total amount of labour exerted on a given territory increases and diminishes according as the population of that territory increases or diminishes, we may word the law thus:—At any given time the population which can exist on a given extent of land, consistently with the attainment of the greatest productiveness of industry possible at that time, is definite. No one, probably, will deny that there might be too few people inhabiting a territory to allow of the attainment of the greatest productiveness of industry possible at the time. If, for instance, there were now in New Zealand only six hundred persons instead of six hundred thousand, no one will doubt

§ 7. POPULATION AND PRODUCTIVENESS.

that the six hundred would not be able to produce so much per head as the six hundred thousand can produce. Six inhabitants, again, would be able to produce still less per head than six hundred; indeed in all probability they would be scarcely able to support life. An increase of population is often one of the most essential requisites for increasing the productiveness of industry. A large population is necessary for the proper division of employments and for carrying out great works. Without a large population it is impossible to have such things as railways, large ships, and mills, to say nothing of art and literature. Hitherto in the world's history it is probable that increase of population has generally, if not almost always, increased, or rather assisted to increase, the productiveness of industry: that is to say, if the population had not increased, it would have been too small to allow of the attainment of the greatest productiveness of industry possible at the time—there would have been 'under-population.'

Some writers have almost, if not quite, denied that there can be too many inhabitants on a given area to allow of the attainment of the greatest productiveness of industry possible at the time. But whether this state of things, which we call 'over-population,' ever does actually occur or not, it is surely clear that it is physically possible. The more people there are on a given area, the less land there is to each person, and if the number of people goes on increasing as it is possible for it to increase, there must come a time sooner or later when there is too little land to each person. Everyone knows that at any given time, or so long as knowledge, the stock of useful material objects, and co-operation remain unaltered, an increase of the labour performed on a field up to a certain point will cause a more than proportionate increase in the produce of that field, and that an increase of the labour expended beyond that point will only cause a less than proportionate increase in the produce. If this were not so, if an increase in the amount of labour performed on a given area were always followed by a more than proportionate, or even a proportionate, increase in the produce, it would be better to grow all the food required by London on one fertile field in the neighbourhood, instead of bringing much of it long distances over sea and land. If the produce of a field increases in the same proportions as the labour executed on it, why not select one fertile field in Middlesex or Kent and employ a hundred, a thousand, nay, a million men on that field, and so make it produce a hundred, a thousand, or a million times as much food as it produces at present? It is evidently just as true in mining as it is in agriculture, that the persons labouring on a given area at a given time must not exceed a certain number, if the productiveness of industry is to be as great as possible; if it were not so, one mine for each mineral might supply whole countries. The fact that a certain amount of space is required for productive labour in other branches of industry is of little practical

§ 7. POPULATION AND PRODUCTIVENESS.

importance as regards the effect of variations of population on the productiveness of all industry taken together, because these branches of industry require very little space compared with agriculture. It is always by acting on agriculture and a few kindred branches of industry that variations of population affect the productiveness of all industry.

To show that both under-population and over-population are possible is not the same thing as showing that either of these things exists now or ever has existed. As there are still large unoccupied tracts of land just as naturally fertile, if not more so, than much of the land which is already cultivated, it is very improbable that the world as a whole has ever suffered from over-population. That some small islands have at times been over-populated is certain, and that considerable areas of large islands and continents have at times been over-populated is extremely probable. The existence of over-population or under-population is not susceptible of exact demonstration: some people think that the productiveness of industry in London would be greater if a plague were to carry off several hundred thousand working Londoners, but they cannot prove that it would be so. Very probably it would be so if the plague judiciously selected all the most incompetent workers, but we must always remember that a mere reduction of population does not necessarily involve a diminution in the number of incompetent workers compared with the number of competent workers.

PART II.

INDIVIDUAL WELFARE UNDER PRIVATE PROPERTY.

§ 1. Complexity introduced by Exchange.

We now leave 'the unchanging laws of political economy,' and pass on to the consideration of economic propositions which can lay no claim to universality, since they presuppose the existence of institutions, laws, and customs which are liable to alteration, and are as a matter of fact continually being altered. We have not, of course, to attempt the impossible task of explaining the causes on which the material welfare of individuals depends under all institutions, laws and customs, but are to confine ourselves to the causes in operation under the institutions which at present exist in this country, and which exist with some not vitally important modifications in the rest of Western Europe, and in America and Australasia.

The two most important institutions as regards the material welfare of individuals in this portion of the world are private property and the State. In this Part we have to discuss the results of the existence of private property.

If private property were established but exchange not practised, the acquisition of material welfare or wealth by individuals would need scarcely any special explanation. The wealth of any individual would be determined in almost exactly the same way as the wealth of mankind or great communities. The wealth of each man would depend upon the produce of his own labour and the utility of that produce to him, and this would depend simply on the amount and quality of the useful material objects in his possession and on the intelligence and industry with which he worked. The useful material objects in his possession would be the identical objects which he had produced by his own labour or obtained by inheritance, bequest, or gift. As he would, under the circumstances assumed, grow his own food, make his own clothes, inhabit and repair his own house, and do everything else for himself, an increase in the productiveness of his own industry would always benefit him, and a decrease in it would always injure him. But private property without exchange is practically impossible, if not altogether inconceivable. Under private property the chief motive which induces men to work is desire to benefit themselves and, in many cases, their families. This motive must inevitably lead to exchange. No human being with an intelligence above that of a brute would ever think of living in isolation on his own property and producing by his own labour every kind of thing which he uses or enjoys. Everyone finds it more conducive to his interest to exchange things, or, as we say, to sell some things and buy others. At present most individuals devote the greater part of their labour to one particular kind of production, and exchange the most of what they produce for the productions of a number of other individuals, each of whom acts in the same way. The reason tailors do not make their own shoes is that they can get shoes more easily by making clothes for shoemakers and others; the reason shoemakers do not make their own clothes is that they can get clothes more easily by making shoes for tailors and others.

Exchange being practised, the comparative wealth of individuals must depend on the terms on which exchanges are effected as well as on the simpler causes, so in order to understand the determination of the relative amounts of wealth enjoyed by individuals we must first have a clear conception of the nature and mechanism of exchange and the various ways of obtaining material welfare or wealth to which exchange gives rise.

§ 2. Kinds of Things which can be Exchanged.

Things which are, under the institution of private property, exchangeable may be divided into three classes:—

1. Useful material objects.
2. The use of such objects for a period of time.
3. Services which do not involve the production of a useful material object.

§ 2. EXCHANGEABLE THINGS.

Everything which is included in any one of these three classes—everything which is exchangeable—we may call a 'commodity,' in the absence of any better term.

As commodities belonging to any one of the three classes or kinds of commodities may be exchanged for commodities which belong to the same class, or to either of the other two classes, we may say that there are six different sorts of exchanges.

(1) One useful material object may be exchanged for another useful material object; e.g. one piece of land may be exchanged for another piece, or a horse for a picture.

(2) The use of a useful material object may be exchanged for the use of another such object; e.g. the use of one house may be exchanged for the use of another, or the use of a ladder for the use of a garden roller.

(3) A service which does not involve the production of a useful material object—a 'pure service' as it is sometimes called—may be exchanged for another such service; e.g. a physician's services may be exchanged for a schoolmaster's.

(4) A useful material object may be exchanged for the use of a useful material object for a period of time; e.g. cattle or corn may be exchanged for the use of a piece of land for a year.

(5) A useful material object may be exchanged for a pure service; e.g. food and clothing may be exchanged for the attendance of a footman.

(6) The use of a useful material object for a period of time may be exchanged for a pure service; e.g. the use of a house may be exchanged for the service of driving a carriage.

§ 3. A Medium of Exchange.

It would evidently be exceedingly awkward if no exchange could take place except where two individuals could directly supply the wants of each other. It does indeed sometimes happen that two individuals can do this. Two landowners, for instance, do sometimes exchange two pieces of land; two house-owners do sometimes exchange the use of two houses for a short period; a doctor and a schoolmaster do sometimes exchange their services; a landowner does sometimes exchange the use of his land for a quantity of the agricultural produce which he requires, and so on. But in many cases it is almost or quite impossible for exchanges 'in kind' to be effected. How, for example, could a physician get bread if he had to be paid for his services in kind, and no bakers happened to fall ill for a time? How could an exchange ever take place between a great artist and a dock-labourer? Obviously society as at present constituted could not exist for a week if all exchanges had to be between individuals who should directly supply each other's wants. As things are, it is evident that there are many more indirect exchanges than direct exchanges. It is much more common for *A* to

§ 3. MEDIUM OF EXCHANGE. 31

supply some want of *B*, who supplies in exchange some want of *C*, who supplies in exchange some want of *D*, who in his turn supplies in exchange some want of *A*, than it is for *A* to supply the wants of *B* in exchange for *B*'s supplying *A*'s wants.

Indirect exchanges are effected by means of 'money.' Each man buys what he wants with money instead of endeavouring to supply some of his productions directly to the persons who supply him with their productions. In its simplest form money is a concrete medium of exchange, a thing which, owing to the customs of a people, anyone will readily accept as a medium, as something between the commodity he is ready to give in exchange and the commodity he wishes to get in exchange, because he knows that every one else will accept it in the same way, so that he will be able to get what he wants by parting with it.

Such a medium of exchange must necessarily belong to the first of the three classes into which commodities are divided; that is, it must be a useful material object, and not either the use of such an object nor a pure service. It is absolutely necessary that a medium of exchange should be capable of being passed from hand to hand— transferred to an almost unlimited number of persons in succession; and neither the use of a material object nor a pure service can be passed from hand to hand. Whether a medium of exchange must be not only a useful material object, but also a material object useful for some other purpose besides that of serving as a medium of exchange, is a question which is not very easy to answer. Experience is not conclusive on the point. It seems to be the case that material objects which are not useful for any other purpose may be made by common consent useful as a medium of exchange, at any rate for a considerable period of time, if their quantity be limited. If more of them can be without difficulty obtained by any one, the quantity of them required to exchange for any other commodity will certainly go on increasing till it reaches infinity. Then of course they must cease to be a medium of exchange.

§ 4. Characteristics of a good Medium of Exchange.

Whether it is possible for material objects which are otherwise useless to be permanently a medium of exchange at all or not, there can be no doubt that they cannot be a good medium of exchange. The general confidence that an object will be taken as a medium of exchange by every one can never be quite so strong when the object is otherwise useless as when it is useful for other purposes.

A good medium of exchange must be durable, portable, and cognizable, as well as useful for other purposes besides that of being a medium of exchange. The longer an object will last without deterioration, the more handy it is to carry, and the more easily recognised it is, the more suitable is it to be a medium of exchange. It is, of course, quite impossible to say whether durability, portability, or cognizability, is the most important, or to estimate how much more of the one will compensate for less of the others.

(1) An object which decays quickly is unsuited to be a medium of exchange, because it would only be readily accepted by people who knew they were going to part with it immediately. No one else would take it. Such commodities as bread and meat could never be at all a good medium of exchange. Cattle, which grow old and die, have sometimes formed a tolerable medium of exchange, but it must be remembered that (to say nothing of the slowness of the deterioration of individual animals) cattle propagate themselves, so that a person would not necessarily lose by having a large number on his hands even for a long time.

(2) The second characteristic of a good medium of exchange, portability, is not such a simple one as it appears at first sight. It is clearly incompatible with fragility or liability to spoil when exposed to the weather; crockery, which would be constantly getting broken, and salt, which would be ruined by rain, would be equally unsuitable. This is plain enough; the difficulty lies in discovering what constitutes portability in relation to size and weight. No such quantity of the medium of exchange as is commonly passed from hand to hand ought to be very bulky or very heavy, or it will encumber and

tire those who have to carry it; but, on the other hand, it ought no less to be not very small or very light, or it will have to be lifted with tweezers and always protected from the wind.

(3) An object of which the quality or genuineness is not easily ascertainable is unsuited to be a medium of exchange, because of the waste of time incurred in testing it by those who accept it, and because of the want of confidence in it which must be engendered by frequent frauds.

The experience of the world appears to show that pieces of certain metals, stamped by persons possessing the public confidence, best fulfil the conditions necessary to make a good medium of exchange. They can be melted down and used for other purposes. They are durable, and their cognizability is more or less certainly secured by the stamp which turns them into 'coin,' and by laws against the issue of counterfeit coin. As to portability, one or other of the several metals commonly coined is always moderately portable. At present we find gold most portable for large purchases, silver for smaller purchases, and bronze for still smaller purchases. For small payments gold would not be bulky enough to be a good medium of exchange, and for very small ones silver would not be bulky enough. On the other hand, bronze would be too bulky except for the smallest payments, and silver would be too bulky for large payments. A silver halfpenny could not be easily handled, and a gold one could not be coined at all, while twenty pounds sterling in bronze pennies would require to be carried in a wheelbarrow, and twenty pounds in silver coins would be a troublesome burden to carry on the person.

§ 5. CREDIT: UNDERTAKINGS TO PAY THE MEDIUM OF EXCHANGE GIVEN INSTEAD OF THE MEDIUM ITSELF.

It would obviously be very inconvenient if the medium of exchange had to be actually passed from hand to hand in large transactions,—if, for instance, every purchaser of a commodity worth £10,000 had to bring the hundredweight and a half of gold sovereigns in a cart, and count them out to the seller of the commodity. Supposing the difficulty of carrying and counting the gold to be got over, there remains a still greater difficulty in the fact that it would be necessary for every purchaser of a commodity to become possessed of its value in gold before he could buy it. Let us suppose that *A* has a house worth £10,000 and that *B* has a mill and *C* a yacht each worth the same sum, and that *A* wants to sell his house and buy *C*'s yacht, while *B* wants to sell his mill and buy *A*'s house, and *C* wants to sell his yacht and buy *B*'s mill. Now if the medium of exchange—gold sovereigns—is to be actually handed over by the purchaser of the house, the mill, and the yacht, before the sellers of those commodities will part with them, then, before the exchanges required can be effected, *A*, *B*, or *C* must have ten thousand sovereigns as well as his commodity worth £10,000. If *A* has the ten thousand sovereigns he will hand them to *C* in exchange for the yacht, *C* will hand them on to *B* in exchange for the mill, and *B* will return them to *A* in exchange for the house. If none of the three have ten thousand sovereigns they cannot effect the exchanges.

Large transactions are now in this country almost invariably effected in a way which dispenses with the possession or handling of the medium of exchange by the purchaser and seller of a commodity. They are accomplished by means of 'credit,' that is, by the seller of the commodity trusting some one's promise to pay a certain amount of the medium of exchange, instead of requiring it to be actually produced. The promise to pay which the seller accepts may be either the verbal or written promise of the purchaser himself, or the written promise of some other person which the purchaser has obtained and transfers to the seller. In the case we have supposed, *A*, instead of producing ten thousand sovereigns, might induce *C* to hand over the yacht in exchange for his promise to pay £10,000 before a given date; then we should have this state of affairs:—

A possesses the house and the yacht, but owes *C* £10,000.

B remains in possession of his mill.

C has A's promise to pay £10,000.

C might now induce B to hand over the mill to him in exchange for A's promise to pay £10,000; then

A has the house and the yacht, and owes B £10,000.

B has A's promise to pay £10,000.

C has the mill, which he wanted.

B will now receive the house from A and in exchange allow A's debt to be cancelled, so that, without any of the medium of exchange ever having been touched by A, B, and C, the required exchanges have been effected:—

A has the yacht
B has the house } Q. E. F.
C has the mill

If A is not trusted sufficiently by B and C to allow of their taking his promise instead of the actual medium of exchange, he may yet be trusted sufficiently by some third person, D, who knows more about his affairs, and whom B and C are willing to trust. Then A will obtain D's written promise to pay £10,000 and hand it to C in exchange for the yacht. C will hand it to B in exchange for the mill, and B will hand it back in exchange for the house to A, who will then get it cancelled. When this third person, D, is a banker, his promises to pay certain amounts of the medium of exchange are called bank notes.

It is often said that bank notes and other written

promises to pay stated amounts of coin are themselves a medium of exchange, but this is by no means the case. When two things are exchanged by the help of a medium of exchange a third commodity equal to them in value is involved. Neither a bank note nor any other piece of paper on which is written a promise to pay a certain number of pounds is such a commodity. Some say, 'a five-pound note enables five pounds in gold to be dispensed with, therefore it must be equal in value to five pounds in gold.' They might as well say 'this man's recovered strength allows him to dispense with his crutches, therefore it must be equal in value to a pair of crutches.' When a man accepts a five-pound note in exchange for some commodity he is not exchanging one commodity worth five pounds for another commodity worth five pounds. He is giving up the possession of one commodity and taking in exchange a piece of paper not worth a farthing, because that piece of paper gives him the right to claim five pounds in gold from the bank. The difference between the medium of exchange and the pieces of paper on which are recorded promises to pay certain amounts of the medium of exchange may be illustrated by considering the effects of the loss or destruction first of a large quantity of gold, and then of a large quantity of written promises to pay gold. If a million pounds in gold be lost, the world is evidently that much the poorer; if paper promises to pay £100,000,000 be burnt, those who promised to pay the £100,000,000 will gain all that the holders of the promises lose.

§ 6. Sources of Individuals' Incomes.

Private property being established and the exchange of commodities made easy by the help of a medium of exchange and credit, then that periodical supply of commodities which we call a man's 'income' 'comes in' to him owing to his possession of property, or owing to his performance of labour, or owing both to his possession of property and his performance of labour.

§ 7. Why Property is a Source of Income.

Since all commodities are produced by labour, there is nothing surprising and nothing that needs explanation in the fact of labour being a source of income. But the question has often been asked, and is still continually asked, 'Why does the mere possession of property enable a man to obtain income?' The true answer to this question is that the existence of income derived from the mere possession of property is a necessary effect of the establishment of private property in useful material objects. Given the existence of private property in useful material objects, such incomes will follow as necessarily as Newton's famous apple fell to the ground. The use of certain material objects is physically necessary for the production of all or nearly all the kinds of pleasures and satisfactions which constitute material welfare. The existence of private property in these material objects means, if it means anything, that the owners or possessors of them are allowed to do what they like with them. This being so, no power on earth can prevent the owners from being able to derive an income from them.

The reason is that from many useful material objects the owner can by his own or others' labour derive pleasures and satisfactions directly for himself. No laws can prevent the owner (provided, of course, that he remains the owner in the full sense of the word) of a house which is comfortable and convenient for him to inhabit, from being better off than if, *ceteris paribus*, he had no such house. Just the same thing is true in the case of land, furniture, books, pictures, clothes, carriages, and innumerable other useful material objects. The possession of land gives a man the power of growing his food upon it, or of sporting on it, or even, if he likes, of admiring the landscapes all by himself; the possession of furniture gives a man the power of lying in a comfortable bed or of sitting in a comfortable chair; the possession of books gives a man the power of amusing or improving his mind; the possession of clothes gives him the power of keeping himself warm, and the possession of carriages (with that of horses) gives him the power of being transported with little fatigue from place to place. It is not in the least necessary that these useful material objects and many others should be lent or let out to other people in order to allow their owners to derive an income from the possession of them. The income which a man derives from using his own property is none the less a perfectly real income because he does not happen to enter its value in pounds on each side of his account book. It would surely be strange to represent a man who sells a house which he used to let, and, with the proceeds of the sale, buys for his own dwelling a house which he used to rent, as diminishing his income by the amount which he used to receive as rent. Evidently his real income is not affected at all, though the rent of the one house will disappear from his annual receipts and the rent of the other from his annual payments. There is, then, nothing wonderful in the fact that the possession of such useful material objects as can be used for the immediate benefit of their owners is a source of income to their owners. The use of such objects benefits the owner if he keeps them and uses them; if he lets them out to another to use, he expects to receive something in exchange for the benefit which he foregoes himself and transfers to the borrower; and the borrower gives something in exchange because he receives the benefit from some one who will not give it him for nothing.

The useful material objects which cannot well be used by their owners form a source of income to their owners in consequence of the existence of useful material objects which can be used by their owners. Useful material objects which can not be made useful immediately to their owners would either not be produced at all, or would not be the property of their present owners, unless they were a source of income, since, if they were not a source of income, every man would prefer to possess other objects which were a source of income. When a man finds himself possessed of some useful material object which he cannot use himself and the use of which he cannot sell to some one else, he immediately proceeds to sell that object and buy something which will be a source of income to him. If, as sometimes happens, he cannot sell the object and it is a perishable article, he allows it to fall into decay. People only own houses which they do not inhabit because they derive house-rent from the possession of them; if there were no house-rent, the houses not inhabited by the owners would be all sold to those who inhabit them, at whatever sacrifice, and no more houses would be built with a view to being let. In exactly the same way, if ship-owners were prevented from receiving an income from the ships which they do not use immediately for their own benefit, existing ships would become the property of some sort of associations which could use them for their own immediate benefit, and in all probability very few new ships would be built; any that were built would be built for the associations. The long and the short of the matter is, that the useful material objects which are not used by their owners form a source of income to their owners because otherwise their owners would prefer to produce and possess things which they could use for their own immediate benefit. A man who has a cotton mill receives something in exchange for the use of it when he grants that use to others, because, if he had not chosen to build or buy a cotton mill, he might have built or bought something, such as a yacht, which he could have used for his own enjoyment.

Many people in all ages, even when they have understood why the mere possession of useful material objects other than coin is a source of income, have found it difficult to explain why the mere possession of 'money' should be a source of income, and still more difficult to understand why 'credit' should be a source of income. Yet it is surely very simple. Whenever money is lent or credit given, the lender of the money or the giver of the credit lends useful material objects to the borrower. If actual coin is lent, then the useful material object, gold, is lent, and there is no more and no less reason why a man should pay for the use of gold than why he should pay for the use of iron or wood. If, on the other hand, no coin is passed from the lender to the borrower, what happens is that the borrower, owing to the credit he has obtained, is able to become possessed of some useful material object which he makes a source of receipts to himself, and therefore has to pay the person who has enabled him to obtain these receipts something in exchange for them.

When it has been proved that private property in useful material objects necessarily leads to income being derived from the mere possession of property, it may be asked whether private property in the produce of labour without private property in material objects could be established, so that labour should be the only source of income. The answer is that private property in the produce of labour without private property in useful material objects, would be certainly impossible in practice, and is perhaps inconceivable in theory; because we know of no way of dividing the alterations made by labour in the form of a material object from the material object itself. No intelligible device for retaining any sort of private property while abolishing incomes derived from the possession of property has ever been discovered.

This point settled, we can now proceed to discuss the various ways in which income may be derived, first from labour, and next from the possession of property.

§ 8. Different ways of deriving Income from Labour.

There are three different ways in which an income may be derived from working. A person may obtain income:—

(1) By producing commodities for his own benefit.

(2) By working in one way or another along with people whom he employs, that is to say, with people who have sold their work to him for payment agreed upon before the work is done.

§ 8. INCOMES FROM LABOUR.

(3) By working for an employer, that is, by selling his work to some one for a payment agreed on before the work is done.

First way:—

The commodities produced by a man who neither 'employs' others nor is 'employed' by another may be used by himself or may be exchanged for other commodities which will be used by himself.

It must always be remembered that exchange of commodities can never prevail to such an extent as to result in each individual producing personally none of the material good things which he enjoys. Every healthy adult does some of his own work; for instance, nearly every man at least puts on his own clothes and cuts his own meat. No increase in the division of employments and exchange of commodities will ever make it possible to procure such satisfactions as that produced by looking at a picture, without some small amount of labour on the part of the person who is to enjoy the satisfactions. It may perhaps be thought that the amount of labour expended directly for the good of the worker himself is at present, in a country like this, altogether unimportant. This is by no means the case. The proportion of such labour to the whole amount is obviously less in this country than in any other, but it is, all the same, a very considerable proportion. Little perhaps of the men's labour is expended directly for their own good; men are much more often engaged in producing commodities for the use of other people than for the use of themselves and their families. But what of the women's labour? Few will doubt that at any rate more than half of the labour of women in this country is expended directly for the good of themselves and their families. As women, on the average, work at least as hard as men, we may therefore conclude that more than a quarter of the labour of the men and women together is expended in producing material good things directly for the use of the producers.

The only reason why the income produced by this labour so often escapes notice is that it is difficult to estimate the value of it in coin. Imaginary cases, of course, may be supposed in which it is easy enough to estimate the value in money of this kind of income. We may, for instance, suppose two teachers, A and B, in these circumstances:—A has £300 a year derived from property and £250 a year derived from the labour of teaching other people's children, and he pays £50 a year to some one else for teaching his children. B has the same amount of income from property as A, obtains £200 a year for teaching other people's children, and personally gives his own children exactly the same quality and amount of teaching that A's children receive. Then it is surely clear that A's and B's incomes are worth the same amount of money, namely, £550 a year. But a simple case like this, which is easy enough to imagine, seldom occurs in practice. Consequently it is usual to overlook the income which an individual produces directly for himself. In the rough-and-ready methods of everyday life *B*'s income would be reckoned as £500 a year only, and he would pay income tax only on that sum, while *A* would pay it on £550.

The income which individuals who are neither employers nor employed obtain by producing commodities which are sold by them when finished for what they will then fetch, is a much less important part of the whole income of the population. It has declined in importance and still is declining. Modern changes have not indeed altogether destroyed the 'independent workman,' as a man is called who works alone or with the assistance of his wife and children, and sells the commodities thus produced, when finished, 'on his own account.' Every one knows of a few instances of 'independent workmen' in trades which do not necessitate the use of machinery or materials which cannot be handled by a single man and his family. Such trades, however, appear to be decreasing, and even in them the livelihood of the independent workman becomes more and more precarious.

Second and third ways:—

From the position of the independent workman to that of the employer on the one hand, and to that of the employed on the other, the transition is in theory extremely gentle. As soon as any one who produces and sells commodities on his own account engages others to assist him in the work of production for sums fixed before the work is done, he begins to derive income from his labour in the second way —he becomes an employer. As soon as he begins to work under an agreement according to which the commodity he produces or helps to produce belongs not to him but to another person who is bound to pay him a fixed sum for his work, he obtains income in the third way—he becomes 'employed' by some one.

It is impossible to divide the population of a country like this into independent workmen on the one hand and employers and employed on the other, because many people work both independently and as employers or employed. A small shoemaker, for instance, may sometimes employ assistance and sometimes not. He will sometimes make boots which he places in his window and sells ready made, and will sometimes make boots under contract with a customer who employs him to make his boots 'to measure.' As for dividing all who are not independent workmen into employers on the one hand and employed on the other, this is still more clearly impossible. Most people are both employers and employed at the same time. A railway company employs a millionaire contractor to make a new line; the contractor employs subcontractors to do different parts of the work; the sub-contractors employ navvies and other workmen; even these last employ various persons at different times to perform services for them (such

§ 8. INCOMES FROM LABOUR.

as cooking) and so nearly all are both employers and employed.

Great confusion of mind commonly exists as to the nature of the exchange which takes place between an employer and those whom he employs. It seems for the most part to have arisen from the erroneous notion that an employer buys labour. This is not at all the case. Labour is not a commodity—it is neither desirable nor exchangeable. What an employer buys is in all cases not the labour of doing a thing but the work done. If you engage a carpenter to make you a box on the terms that you shall provide him with the necessary materials, lend him the necessary tools, and pay him half-a-crown when the box is finished, then you will pay the half-crown not in exchange for his labour, but in exchange for the making of the box. As it would be popularly expressed with equal brevity and accuracy, you pay half-a-crown 'for the carpenter's work.' Before, you had wood, nails, hinges, a lock, tools, and half-a-crown: now, you still have the tools (a little the worse for wear) but instead of the wood, nails, hinges, and lock, in their former condition, you have a box. You have got no 'labour' to show for your half-crown; what you have got in exchange for it and the wear and tear of your tools is the difference between the materials of which the box is made and the finished box; this difference is not the carpenter's labour but the result of his labour. When we say that it is the carpenter's 'work,' we use the word 'work' not as equivalent to 'labour,' but as equivalent to the result of labour, just as when we call a book a 'work' or when we say 'this is bad work.'

Whether a man is paid 'by time' or 'by the piece' he is equally paid for the result of his labour and not for his labour itself. It might be thought that when a contract is made to pay a man so much 'for a day's labour' instead of so much for a definite piece of work, it must be his labour that is bought. But a contract to pay a man so much a day 'for his labour' is in reality only a contract to pay him so much for a piece of work very roughly defined. No one agrees to pay a man anything for a day's labour unless he agrees either explicitly or implicitly not only to labour for a certain number of hours, but also in a certain way, or as he may from time to time be directed, which is practically equivalent to agreeing to labour with a certain amount of effect—to doing an inaccurately defined quantity of work. For instance, if you engage a man to dig, you expect him to dig a reasonable quantity of ground in the day; if he insisted on simply turning over the same spadeful again and again the law would not compel you to give him the wages agreed on, however industriously the man might have laboured over his one spadeful. Accordingly, what you buy is not the labour of digging but the difference between undug ground and ground which is dug.

Another widespread delusion as to the nature of

the exchange between employer and employed is the notion that an employer 'advances' wages to those whom he employs. It is as a matter of fact the exception and not the rule for wages to be paid in advance. As a rule work is only paid for after it is done; those who are paid by time are paid when the day, week, month, or quarter ends, and those who are paid by the piece are paid after they have finished each piece of work, and not before. If it be said that the statement that employers advance wages does not mean that they pay for work before it is done, but only that they pay for it before the commodity which is being produced is finished, the answer is that even then it would not be anything like universally true. In innumerable cases the commodity which an employer sells is not only finished but in the hands of his customers before the wages of those who are employed in its production are paid. Take, for instance, the case of the wages paid by the printer of a daily newspaper: how much of these is paid before the newspaper is finished? The wages which are paid weekly on Saturday evening will be payments for assisting to produce papers which were issued from the press complete half a day, one and a half, two and a half, three and a half, four and a half, five and a half days before the wages are paid. The wages which are paid quarterly will be payments for assisting to produce commodities which were finished, on the average, still longer before the wages are paid. The only vestige of a foundation which can be found for the notion that wages are commonly advanced is the fact that employers often pay those whom they employ for assisting to produce a commodity before their customers have paid them for that commodity. This is not of course always the case; for instance, a railway company obtains its passenger receipts before it pays its passenger guards, engine-drivers, and porters. When it is the case, the advance is made by the employer not to those whom he employs, but to those whom he allows to have the commodity before they have paid for it.

What an employer does before the work is done is not to pay for it but to agree to pay a certain sum for it when it is done. It is this agreement which makes the difference between an employer and a mere buyer of a ready-made commodity. When a man buys flowers in pots from a florist, or potatoes from a green-grocer, he is not an employer. When he agrees to pay some one twenty-five shillings a week for keeping his garden in order he is an employer. It is not necessary in order to make a person an employer that he should supply either materials or tools; in some employments neither are needed, in others the employed supply one or the other or both.

The fact that there is nothing occult or mysterious in the nature of the exchange which takes place between employer and employed may perhaps be made clear by comparing a business as conducted by an ordinary employer with the same business as carried on by an association of independent workmen working on its own account. Let us imagine a factory belonging to an ordinary employer who employs a hundred workpeople and in an average year sells the total produce of the factory for £10,000. Let us further suppose that these £10,000, the gross receipts, are thus divided:—

	£	£
Materials, etc. bought	500	
Wages of 100 workpeople	7500	
Employer's total working expenses		8000
Interest on employer's capital (chiefly payment for the use of the factory)	1500	
Employer's profit over and above interest on his capital	500	
Employer's total profit		2000
Total		10000

Now to turn this business into a business carried on by an association of independent workmen, all that is necessary is that the employed and the employer should associate themselves together, carry on the production, and sell the produce in the name of the association. As regards the management, the difference will be that the supreme power will be in the hands of a democracy instead of in those of an autocrat, but of course the democracy may, if it chooses, delegate a great deal of this power to one person. As regards the distribution of the gross receipts, the difference will be that instead of the employer paying fixed amounts to the other producers and keeping what is left for himself, the association, after paying for materials and other things which it has bought, and probably after paying a fixed sum for the use of the factory, will divide the remainder of the gross receipts between the producers in proportions agreed upon before the work was begun. Possibly even the owner of the factory might agree to accept a proportion of the receipts instead of a fixed sum, but whether he be paid a fixed sum or a proportion makes no material difference. The most important result of this change in the method of dividing the gross receipts will be that the old employer (whom we suppose to be retained as manager to the association) will be less pecuniarily interested, and the old employed (who are now members of the association) will be more pecuniarily interested, in the economical working of the particular factory in question. Under the old system if the work and management had been so slack that the total produce sold only for £8,000, the employer and owner of the factory would get nothing, and if the work and management had been so good that the produce sold for £12,000, the employer and owner would get £4,000, while the employed would receive in both cases the same wages, since the employer, whether he did well or ill, would have to pay much the same wages as were paid by other employers and no more.

§ 8. INCOMES FROM LABOUR.

Under the new system the £8,000, £10,000 and £12,000 would be thus distributed:—

	£	£	£
Materials, etc. bought	500	500	500
Owner of factory (fixed sum)	1500	1500	1500
Ex-employer (as manager) $\frac{1}{16}$ of remainder	375	500	625
Ex-employed (now members) $\frac{15}{16}$	5625	7500	9375
Totals	8000	10000	12000

Before concluding this section it is desirable to say something about the different names applicable to income earned by labour in different ways. When a person is employed and his gross receipts from his employer or employers are almost the same as his net receipts from the same source we call his earnings his 'wages' or 'salary.' But if his gross receipts are much greater than his net receipts, if, that is to say, a considerable part of his gross receipts is payment for the use of instruments of production belonging to him or hired by him, or merely reimburses him for the cost of materials, then what he earns by his labour (which will be part or the whole of his net receipts) is called 'profit.' Similarly, the earnings of the labour of an employer and the earnings of the independent workman who sells commodities ready made to his customers are called 'profit.' The earnings obtained by labour directed immediately to the benefit of the worker himself appear to have no particular designation. Thus we see that the term 'wages' is applicable only to one portion of the earnings of labour—a large portion it is true, but not an overwhelmingly large one. It is an abuse of terms to call the whole of the earnings of labour 'wages' and to speak of 'profits' as if they comprised nothing but income derived from the possession of property.

§ 9. Different ways of deriving Income from Property.

There may be said to be three different ways in which a person can derive income from the possession of property. He may derive income from his property:—

(1) By using it himself either alone or in conjunction with others.

(2) By keeping in his possession property of a certain kind till it is ready for use or wanted.

(3) By selling the use of his property to others for fixed periodical payments.

First way:—

There are several methods by which a man may obtain income by using his own property himself.

In the first place he may use it either by himself, or in conjunction with people employed by him, in producing material goods for his own personal benefit. This is the way in which a man derives income from the possession of the house he lives in and the carriage he drives about in. It often escapes attention because, as it is not exchanged for money, it does not commonly appear in account books and much of it escapes income tax. To estimate its practical importance we have only to think of the parks and gardens, houses, furniture, clothes, carriages and horses which are used by their owners for their immediate benefit. In framing an accurate estimate of the income of an individual, we surely ought to know whether he is living in the midst of beautiful grounds in a fine house with sumptuous and tasteful furniture, clothed in gorgeous attire, or in a single roomed tenement in a dirty court, with no furniture but a broken chair, dressed in filthy rags. Obviously, if we wish to compare accurately the incomes of two individuals, we must consider the value of the use of the property which they use for their own benefit as well as other parts of their income. As has been already pointed out, it is only owing to the fact that useful material objects can be used by their owner for his own immediate benefit that income can be derived from the possession of property at all.

In the second place, a man may use his own property, either alone or in conjunction with persons employed by him, in producing commodities for exchange. The independent workman and the employed worker obtain income in this way from the possession of the tools which they use. Clearly these workers will get more profit and wages when they own their instruments of production than when they do not; a cabman who possesses his cab is better off than one who does not, and so on. The employer similarly derives income from the possession of the materials and instruments of production which he uses in conjunction with those whom he employs. Of the total profit or amount of net receipts which employers obtain from their businesses a part consists of the earnings of their labour and another part of income derived from the possession of the useful material objects—such as factories or ships—used. Of course individual employers often manage so badly that they not only get nothing for their labour but nothing also for the use of their property, and so from one point of view it seems as if an employer's profits depended entirely on the amount and quality of his labour. But those employers who can get nothing for the use of their property are people who misuse rather than use their property; when we say that a man can obtain income by using his own property we mean that he can obtain income by using his property in a business-like manner.

Second way :—

It is well known that some people derive income from the possession of property by keeping useful material objects till they are ready for use or till they are wanted. Such things rise in value as time goes on, and the increment of value is part of their owners' income, although it may not be

§ 9. INCOMES FROM PROPERTY.

'realised' as stockbrokers say, that is, sold for money, every year. If a man has a cellar of port wine or a plantation of trees the annual increment of the value of these things is evidently part of his annual income; if he likes to spend it, he can do so without decreasing his property, and if he does not choose to spend it, he is engaged in a form of saving and is thereby adding to his property.

In considering this way of obtaining income from the possession of property we are apt to think only of such property as port-wine or trees, because it is only in such cases that the property has to be kept so long that the increment of value is large enough to be unmistakable. But reflection will convince us that the same increment of value occurs in the case of all useful material objects which are undergoing the ordinary course of production, and that consequently income may be obtained simply by possessing useful material objects while they are still not ready for use. In the case of an article in the maker's hands, the increment of value owing to its being nearer in time to completion is completely dwarfed, as a rule, by the increment of value which takes place owing to the article being nearer completion as regards the work done on it. But it exists; an article complete and ready for use will sell for more than the sum for which it would sell six months before it was finished added to the cost of finishing it. There is surely nothing surprising or anomalous in this. No one expects a house 'with possession in six months' to sell for as much as an exactly similar house 'with immediate possession,' because it is obvious that the purchaser of the house with immediate possession will have six months longer enjoyment of the use of the house than the purchaser of the house with possession in six months. In just the same way no one ought to expect a commodity which will not be ready for use till six months have elapsed, to sell now for the same price as it will sell for at the end of the six months; if it were now offered at that price no one would buy it, because all would prefer to possess in the meantime some commodity the use of which could be enjoyed, and then to buy the other commodity at the end of the six months.

Third way:—

We now come to what is perhaps the most obvious and simple method of obtaining income from the possession of property, the method adopted by those who sell the use of their property to others for periodical payments, or, as it may be shortly expressed, who lend their property for profit.

The periodical payments which a man receives in consequence of having lent his property have several names each of which is more or less appropriated to payments for the use of a single class of property. Payments received periodically for the loan of immovable useful material objects such as land, houses or railways, are commonly called 'rent.' Economists, indeed, have often endeavoured to restrict the term 'rent' to payments for the use

§ 9. INCOMES FROM PROPERTY.

of land alone, but this is a futile attempt. If the periodical payments made by the tenant of a house to the owner are not to be called 'rent' what are they to be called? Moreover it is not practically possible to divide actual payments made for the use of immovable objects and the land they stand on into two parts, and say 'so much is paid for the use of the land' and 'so much for the use of what is on the land;' payments for the use of land are generally quite inextricably entangled with payments for the use of buildings, hedges, ditches, drains, roads, railway cuttings and embankments, and all sorts of immovable useful objects. We may take it then that rent is the term properly applied to periodical payments made by the 'tenants' of immovable property to the 'landlords' or owners of the property. The lender of such property is usually said to 'let' it to the borrower, and the borrower is said to 'take' or 'rent' it. In a few cases the lender of immovable property is sometimes said to 'let it on hire,' and the borrower is said to 'hire' it; a room or a hall may be 'hired' and the Authorised Version speaks of St. Paul dwelling 'in his own hired house.' These cases are exceptional.

The payments periodically made by the borrowers of movable property other than money to the owners of the property commonly go by the name of 'hire.' Hire is paid, for instance, to the lender of a boat, a carriage, a sewing machine, or a steam roller.

The payments which are made by the borrowers to the lenders of money are called 'interest.'

Rent, hire, and interest generally, it must be noticed, include something besides the income which the lender obtains because he owns the property lent. Everyone knows that there is generally a difference, great or small, between the gross rent or hire of a commodity and its net rent or hire. There is also, though this is not so generally recognised, a difference in most cases between the gross and the net interest received by the lenders of money.

In the case of rent and hire, a large proportion of the difference between the gross receipts of the lender and the income which he receives in consequence of owning property, usually consists of the amount which he has to spend on repairs of the commodity lent, or which he has to lay by in order that when that commodity is quite worn out he may be able to replace it by a new one. Most useful material objects require occasional repairs and occasional renewal, and the expense of these repairs and renewals is in most cases borne by the proprietors and not by the borrowers. The cases in which the object lent requires neither repair nor renewal, and those in which the borrower is bound to execute all repairs and renewals, are the exception rather than the rule. No payment for repairs or renewals is ever included in interest, not because coin does not require repair or renewal, for it does wear out, but because the borrower of

§ 9. INCOMES FROM PROPERTY.

money does not undertake to return to the lender the same money as he borrowed but other money of the legal standard, and therefore presumably as good as that which he borrowed. If he borrows a hundred sovereigns or twenty five-pound notes, he does not undertake to return at the end of a given period the same hundred sovereigns or the same twenty five-pound notes. He contracts a debt which can be liquidated by the payment of any hundred sovereigns not below standard weight, or by the payment of any Bank of England notes for £100. The lender can demand no more and need be satisfied with no less than this. Obviously then, there is no room for a payment for repairs or renewals; the borrower of money is in much the same position as the borrower of some other commodity who undertakes to return it in exactly the same condition as that in which it was when he borrowed it.

Gross interest, however, as well as gross rent and hire, usually includes, beside the income obtained from his property by the proprietor of the things lent, a payment for labour performed by him or by people employed by him. The labour of those who lend money to such institutions as governments and banks is too small to be appreciable, and so their receipts may be considered as all clear income derived from the possession of property. The labour of those who lend large sums to individuals or companies for long periods is not very great. But the labour of those who lend small sums for short periods to persons whose solvency is not very apparent is considerable in relation to the total amount lent, and is moreover often of a character not calculated to make the lender very popular. As for commodities other than money, it is obvious that a good deal of labour must be incurred in the business of lending most of them. Payments for labour performed by the lender himself, and not by people employed by him, will of course form a part of his net profit or gain and be part of his income, but they will be income derived from his labour, not from his possession of property, and therefore must not, strictly speaking, be included in the net rent, hire, or interest.

§ 10. THE COMPARATIVE SIZE OF INDIVIDUALS' INCOMES DEPENDENT ON VALUES.

We may now proceed to the consideration of that which is commonly called by economists 'the distribution of wealth.' This phrase is very apt to be misleading. It can only be properly used when it is clearly understood, not only that it means the distribution of income, and not the distribution of property, but also that it does not imply that the material welfare or the income of the individuals of whom a nation consists is first produced, so to speak, in a lump and then divided or parcelled out among them. It is true that each individual's income is generally produced by the co-operation of many individuals, but it is not true that the co-operation carried on by means of exchange creates a joint or aggregate income which has to be divided among the co-operators.

To avoid the use of the misleading expression, we may say that we have now to consider the causes on which the relative or comparative size of individuals' incomes depend, so far as private property and exchange are concerned. To put it broadly, we want to know why some are rich and others poor.

No demonstration is needed to show that where exchange is largely practised the size of an individual's income, compared with the size of other individuals' incomes, necessarily depends upon the value of the produce of his labour, added to the value of the use of his property compared with the value of the produce of other individuals' labour, added to the value of the use of their property. No one, it may be supposed, will be in the least inclined to deny that when a person obtains an income which is large compared with other men's incomes, it is because the produce of his labour or the use of his property has a great value compared with the produce of other men's labour and the use of their property. In order, therefore, to discover what settles the comparative amounts of income obtained by different individuals, we must first inquire what 'the value of a commodity' means, how it is measured so that we can describe it as great or small, and what the causes are which make it great or small.

F

§ 11. THE VALUE OF A COMMODITY.

The value of a given quantity of a commodity in some other commodity is the quantity of the second commodity for which the given quantity of the first commodity is exchanged; thus the value of a quantity of one commodity in another commodity may be roughly defined. So, if a quarter of wheat is exchanged for two pounds, then the value of a quarter of wheat in gold sovereigns is two sovereigns, and if we like so to express it, we may say that the value of wheat in English coin is two pounds the quarter. But if we are striving after accuracy, we soon perceive that there is a good deal of indefiniteness about the expression 'is exchanged.' Everyone knows that a quantity of a commodity is often exchanged for more or less than its value in some other commodity; for instance, a house may be exchanged for £8,000 in consequence of the owner's supineness or ignorance of the state of the house market, when its real value is £10,000. To attain greater accuracy, then, we may substitute for 'is exchanged' some such phrase as 'is being exchanged between two persons equally capable and desirous of promoting their own interests.' Here we fall into another difficulty, since it is clear that a commodity has a value in another commodity not only when it is actually being exchanged, but at all times; a quarter of wheat has its value in pounds at 1 A.M. as well as when Mark Lane is busiest, and a house has a

§ 11.   THE VALUE OF A COMMODITY.   67

value in pounds at other times besides the moment when the agreement for its sale or even for the sale of a similar house is being made. It may perhaps be objected that the value of a commodity in some other commodity when no exchanges are being made is only an 'estimated value.' True; but if the estimate is a correct estimate, the estimated value will be also the real value of the commodity. The difficulty of estimating the height of a mountain correctly without any instruments does not prevent the mountain having a height till the instruments are fetched. No more does the difficulty of estimating in what proportions two commodities will be exchanged by two equally business-like and well-informed individuals prevent the one commodity from having a value in the other, although the two persons are not at the time transacting an exchange. Our definition must therefore be corrected and enlarged so as to read:— The value of a given quantity of a commodity in some other commodity is the quantity of the second commodity for which the given quantity of the first commodity is being exchanged between two persons equally desirous and capable of promoting their own interests, or, if no such exchange is taking place, it is the quantity of the second commodity for which a perfect judge or valuer estimates that the given quantity of the first commodity would at the time be exchanged between two such persons, supposing an exchange took place in the ordinary course of business. It must be understood that the exchange need not take place directly between the two commodities, but may be carried out through the help of the medium of exchange. If, for instance, we say that the value of a quarter of wheat in coal of a certain quality is at a certain place and time two tons, we do not necessarily mean that a quarter of wheat is directly exchanged for two tons of coal, nor that our perfect valuer would imagine such a thing happening; we should probably only mean that a quarter of wheat and two tons of coal are each exchanged, or estimated to exchange, for the same amount of some third commodity.

The value of a commodity is always a quantity of some other commodity. Often, it is true, statements are made about 'the value of such and such a commodity' without any other commodity being mentioned. Sometimes this merely indicates confusion of mind; for instance, when a person asserts that gold has now a larger value than it had twenty years ago, and does not know exactly in what commodities or combination of commodities he is reckoning the value of gold, his mind must be in a state of confusion, and his assertion is meaningless. Sometimes 'the value of a commodity' (other than pounds sterling) simply means its value in pounds or gold sovereigns. Sometimes by 'the value of a commodity' is understood its value in other somewhat similar commodities; if, for instance, we say that 'the value of wheat is great,' we may mean that a quarter of wheat is exchanged for more than a quarter of oats, barley, or rye; and if we say 'the value of this clock is great,' we may mean that its value in ordinary clocks is great, that it might be exchanged for more than one ordinary clock.

§ 12. The Comparison or Measurement of the Values of Commodities.

We do not often in practice estimate the value of a commodity in anything except the medium of exchange. We speak of the value of a house being a certain number of gold sovereigns or 'pounds,' but we do not speak of its value in coal. The existence of a medium of exchange in the shape of pounds makes it convenient to estimate the value of the house in pounds and the value of coal in pounds, if we wish to know how much coal the house will exchange for. If the owner of the house wishes to exchange it for coal, he will sell it for pounds and buy coal with the pounds; consequently neither he nor any one else will think of the value of the house in coal. No one will say, 'The value of that house is twelve thousand tons of such and such coal at such and such a place'; they will say, 'The value of the house is £10,000, and the value of a ton of coal is sixteen-and-eightpence.'

It is a mistake to say that the value of a commodity in the medium of exchange is just the same thing as its 'price.' Every commodity has a value in the medium of exchange, but not every commodity has a price; a house may be worth

£10,000, but if the owner does not offer to sell it for a certain sum, and if no one offers to buy it for a certain sum, it has no price. No commodity has a price unless some one offers to buy or sell it for a specified sum. Merely offering it for sale does not give it a price; when an article is offered for sale by auction the auctioneer may be heard entreating his audience 'Give me a price, please.' Moreover a commodity cannot have more than one value in the medium of exchange, whereas it often has two prices, 'buyers' price' and 'sellers' price.' It constantly happens that the owner of a commodity offers to sell it at one price while some one else is ready to buy it at a lower price; one of these prices must, and both of them may, differ from the real value of the commodity in the medium of exchange.

When it is the custom to estimate the values of all commodities in one particular commodity, that commodity is made thereby a common measure of the relative value of different commodities. Of course any commodity may, if people choose, be used as a measure of value. If a given quantity of some commodity will exchange for two tons of coal, that commodity is twice as valuable as a commodity the same quantity of which will only exchange for one ton of coal; a commodity which will exchange for many tons of coal is more valuable than one which will exchange for few, just as a commodity which will exchange for many gold sovereigns is more valuable than one which will exchange for few. But the fact remains that the medium of exchange is the only commodity which is ordinarily used as a measure for comparing the relative value of two or more commodities.

The medium of exchange and every other commodity will only serve to compare the value of two commodities at one and the same time. The fact that some commodity is now worth two pounds shows that it is twice as valuable as a commodity which is now worth one pound, but it does not show that it is twice as valuable now as a commodity which was worth one pound fifty years ago was then. Attempts used constantly to be made to find something which should serve as a measure of value between commodities at different times. These attempts were necessarily futile. The value of a given quantity of one commodity in another commodity, the value, for instance, of a quarter of wheat in gold, can only be discoverable when exchange takes place, and no exchanges of commodities can by any possibility take place between people living at different times. A quarter of wheat in 1888 can have a value in gold in 1888, but a quarter of wheat in 1888 cannot have a value in gold in 1788. Each time must stand by itself, and we must always remember that it is never more true to say that the value of gold in wheat has risen than to say that the value of wheat in gold has fallen; 'the value of A in B has risen' and 'the value of B in A has fallen' are identical statements.

§ 13. Causes on which the comparative Values of Commodities Depend.

According to a theory which at one time obtained the support of great economists, it was held that the comparative values of different commodities, or the proportions in which commodities are exchanged, depended on the comparative quantity of labour which had been directly and indirectly expended in producing that part of the supply of each commodity which had been produced under the most unfavourable circumstances. It was held, for example, that if it required exactly the same amount of direct and indirect labour to raise two quarters of wheat from the worst wheat-growing land necessarily used, as to extract one ounce of gold from the worst gold mine used, then two quarters of wheat would exchange for one ounce of gold. This theory was confessedly incomplete, for it was only put forward as applicable to 'freely produced' commodities, commodities which could be produced in indefinite quantities by labour. It did not profess to explain what settles the comparative value of commodities of which no more can be produced by any amount of labour, such as the works of dead artists; nor did it explain why an acre of land in certain situations should be worth many thousand pounds, although no labour had ever been expended on it, or although every trace of past labour had been removed from it; nor did it explain why the use of

§ 13. DETERMINATION OF VALUES. 73

an article for a period of time should be exchangeable for the produce of labour. For the comparative values of these things other rules had to be invented. But besides the fact that it only professed to be applicable to one rather ill-defined set of commodities, the theory which based value on quantity of labour was flagrantly untrue, even in relation to those commodities to the case of which it was supposed to be applicable.

Everyone knows that, as a matter of fact, some kinds of labour are so much more highly paid than others that it is impossible to believe that the comparative value of given quantities of freely produced commodities is regulated by the comparative quantity of labour expended in producing them under the most unfavourable circumstances. No one really doubts that a ten pound watch represents less direct and indirect labour than ten pounds' worth of wheat grown on the worst wheat-growing land used. The difficulty is not to be lightly leapt over by saying, 'Oh, but of course skilled labour counts as equal to six times unskilled labour,' or 'skilled labour must be reduced to its equivalent in unskilled.' Neither six hours nor any particular number of hours of unskilled labour is 'equivalent' to one hour of skilled labour; it is true that in some cases unskilled labour can do in a long time what skilled labour can do in a short time, but in many cases, if not in most cases, no amount of unskilled labour can do in any length of time what skilled labour can do in a short time. There is consequently no way of 'reducing skilled labour to its equivalent in unskilled.'

A much better account of the causes which settle the comparative value of given quantities of different commodities is that which is popularly expressed by saying that those causes are 'supply and demand.' The two factors on which the comparative value of given quantities of all commodities depend are their comparative plentifulness, and the comparative estimation in which they, or, in the case of material objects, the satisfactions which are ultimately obtained by using them, are held by human beings. So long as these two factors remain the same, values remain the same; if either of them vary, values will vary, unless the other vary so as to counteract the variation in the first. So long as the comparative estimation in which different commodities (or the satisfactions ultimately obtained by using them) are held remain the same, a diminution in the comparative plentifulness of any commodity will raise the amount of any other commodities for which a given quantity of it will exchange, and an increase in its comparative plentifulness will reduce that amount. So long, again, as the comparative plentifulness of different commodities remains the same, a diminution in the comparative estimation in which any particular commodity (or the satisfaction ultimately obtained by using it) is held will reduce the amount of any other commodities for which a given quantity of it will exchange, and an increase in the comparative estimation in which it is held will increase that amount. Illustrations of these rules will readily occur to every mind. If the price of wheat is higher than usual, to what is the fact commonly attributed? To a deficient harvest; wheat is less plentiful than usual, and gold is as plentiful as usual, and accordingly the value of a quarter of wheat in gold is higher than usual. If anyone thinks that the value of an ounce of gold measured in some other commodities is increasing, to what does he attribute it? Either to an increase in the estimation in which gold money is held, or to a decrease in the plentifulness of gold compared with that of the other commodities (which, of course, is the same thing as an increase in the plentifulness of those other commodities compared with that of gold). If any particular class of traders cannot sell the commodities in which they deal at a high enough price to give them what they consider 'a fair profit,' of what do they most often complain? Of the 'competition' to which they are subjected, which means the number of people who are offering for sale the same commodities as they are offering. If anyone hears that on a certain occasion a gallon of water was sold for £5, what inference does he draw? That water must have been very scarce on that occasion. If ostrich feathers suddenly fell in price, to what would this be most probably attributed? To ostrich feathers 'having gone out of fashion,' that is, not being held in the same estimation as before. The most common cause of a fall in the value of a commodity measured in some other commodity is, of course, an increase in its comparative plentifulness resulting from some invention which increases the powers of its producers.

Variations of value caused by changes in the comparative plentifulness of different commodities and the comparative estimation in which they (or the satisfactions ultimately obtained by means of them) are held, have often been considered as merely 'temporary fluctuations,' so that it was supposed there must be some deeper causes than mere 'supply and demand' for settling the normal as opposed to the temporary market value of different commodities. This opinion appears to have had its origin in the observation of the fact that generally, in the case of freely produced commodities, an alteration in the value of commodities leads to an alteration in their comparative plentifulness, since, if the value of a commodity rises, more of it is produced, and if it falls less of it is produced, and consequently the value has a tendency to revert to what it was before. This fact, however, does not make it at all less true that the actual proportions in which commodities do exchange for one another, whether those proportions happen to be what are supposed to be the normal proportions or not, depend on the comparative plentifulness of the different commodities and the estimation in which they or the satisfactions resulting from their use are held.

The reason why alterations in the comparative

§ 13. DETERMINATION OF VALUES. 77

plentifulness of different commodities cause alterations in their comparative value is that though human desires for all kinds of pleasures taken together are practically insatiable, the desire for any particular pleasure is not usually by any means insatiable. However hungry or desirous of eating a man may be, he cannot eat to an unlimited extent; set him at a plentiful table and at length he will rise satisfied, and no more food would then be of any use to him. However cold a man may be, he may be warmed till he is fain to take coals off the fire, or open the window, or strip off his great coat; his desire for warmth is satisfied. More refined wants are not quite so easily satisfied, but they, too, soon begin to approach satisfaction. Perhaps it would be difficult to conceive a man with such an enormous collection of pictures that the possession of them became at last more of a weariness than a delight to him, because the pride of possession, like ambition, may be supposed to grow by what it feeds on, but of the actual pleasure of looking at pictures a surfeit can easily be taken. Probably, again, no one could bear to hear the most beautiful music all day long. At any rate, the more a person has even of a refined pleasure the less he desires an additional given quantity of it. The consequence of these facts is, of course, that the quantity of any commodity which any individual will buy is affected by its price, by, to speak more accurately, the quantity of other commodities which he will have to give in exchange for a given quantity of it. So, if it is required to induce an individual or a number of individuals to buy more of any commodity, the shortest way of accomplishing that end is usually to lower the price at which it is offered for sale; there may be some people who will not buy any more of it in consequence of the reduction, but some of the old buyers are almost sure to buy more, and if the commodity is not a first necessary of life, some people who before bought none of it will now buy some of it.

An illustration will perhaps make the whole question more clear. Let us suppose that a publisher can sell 1,000 copies of a particular book at two shillings each, that he can only sell 500 copies if he sells them at three shillings each, and only 250 if he sells them at five shillings each. This does not mean that the first 250 copies will be more useful absolutely than the next 250, and that the first 500 will be more useful absolutely than the last 500. What it does mean is that there are 250 persons ready to sacrifice at least five shillings' worth of other commodities in order to obtain the book, that there are another 250 persons who are not ready to sacrifice five shillings' worth of other commodities to obtain the book, but are ready to sacrifice at least three shillings' worth, and that there are 500 more who, though not willing to sacrifice three shillings' worth, are ready to sacrifice at least two shillings' worth of other commodities in order to obtain the book. The last copy, which would not have been bought if the price had been 2s. 1d., may be just as useful, give just as much pleasure to the poor man who buys it as the first copy, which would have been bought if the price had been five pounds, gives to the rich man who buys it. It is therefore not less useful absolutely, but it is less useful compared with a given quantity of other commodities; the poor purchaser hesitates between buying the book and buying a pound of two shilling tea; it is therefore not much more useful to him in his estimation than that pound of tea; the rich purchaser, on the other hand, who would have given five pounds for the book if he could not have got it for less, thinks the book more useful to him than thirty additional pounds of three-and-fourpenny tea.

§ 14. The Comparison of Incomes.

The size of a man's income compared with the size of other men's incomes depends, as has already been observed, on the value of the produce of his labour and the use of his property compared with the value of the produce of other men's labour and the use of their property. The produce of a man's labour and the use of his property form a collection of commodities, and thus we can compare the size of several incomes by taking the various commodities of which the several collections consist, setting down their values in quantities of some one commodity, adding up the items, and then comparing the totals. The one commodity may, of course, be any commodity, but in practice it is always the medium of exchange.

In ordinary life, as everyone knows, incomes are commonly considered as consisting of a certain number of coins. A's income 'is,' it is said, 'two hundred pounds,' and B's 'is four hundred pounds,' and so on. In this way of speaking the measure of the income is put for the income itself. A's income really consists of a whole collection of commodities, of which the total value in pounds is two hundred, and B's income really consists of another collection, the total value of which in pounds is four hundred. We are so accustomed to estimate and compare incomes by estimating their total values in the medium of exchange, that we have fallen into the habit of talking as if incomes consisted of amounts of the medium of exchange.

Care must be taken not to expect too much from this method of comparing incomes. In the first place, we must not suppose that the size of incomes, as measured by their value in some one commodity, indicates exactly the amount of material comfort obtainable by the receivers of incomes. The fact that A's income is estimated at £200 and B's at £400 does not necessarily imply that B is twice as comfortable as A; probably, though not necessarily, he will be more comfortable than A, but it is improbable that he will be twice as comfortable. It is still more improbable that a man with a million pounds a year will be one thousand times as comfortable as a man with a thousand pounds a year. We are only justified in saying that *B*'s income is double *A*'s because *B* can, if he chooses, have twice as much of every commodity as *A* has; of course he will not choose to do so, because, to take the simplest case, if he ate double the quantity of food which *A* eats, he would in all probability be not comfortable at all, but very ill. In the second place, estimation of the value of incomes in some one commodity is useless for the purpose of comparing the size of incomes obtained at different times, or at the same time in places which have very little or no commercial dealing with each other. An income of £300 a year now may or may not be as great as an income of £300 a year in 1870, and an income of forty pounds a year in England might be more or less than an income in a rarely-visited island of the Pacific which would there be worth forty sovereigns.

Incomes existing at different times, or in places between which no commercial communication prevails, cannot be compared except in a very rough way. If we want to compare an income of £300 now with an income of £300 a year in 1870, the only way to do it is to consider whether with £300 now a man can get all the commodities which men with £300 a year in 1870 used then habitually to get with that sum. If he can get those commodities and nothing more, then we are justified in saying that an income of £300 a year now is equal to an income of £300 a year in 1870. If he can

G

get the commodities which men with £350 a year used to be able to get in 1870, then we are justified in considering an income of £300 a year now as equal to an income of £350 a year in 1870. But the fact of £300 a year now being equal to £300 or to £350 a year in 1870 would not in the least prove a present income of £3,000 to be equal to an income of £3,000 or £3,500 in 1870. People who have £3,000 a year do not buy the same commodities in the same proportions as those who have only £300, and so it might very well happen that the average person with £3,000 a year now might not be able to buy all the commodities which the average person with £3,000 a year bought in 1870, although the average person with £300 a year now could buy all the commodities which the average person with £300 could buy in 1870.

§ 15. Causes which determine the Comparative Size of the Incomes individuals derive from Labour.

The size of a man's income compared with the size of other men's incomes depends on the value of the produce of his labour added to the value of the use of his property, compared with the value of the produce of their labour added to the value of their property. The comparative value of commodities depends on their comparative plentifulness and the comparative estimation in which they (or the satisfactions ultimately obtained by using them) are held. These two propositions, taken together, form a foundation for a complete theory as to the causes which settle the comparative amounts of income which can be obtained by doing work and owning property, since both work done, or produce of labour, and property are commodities.

When several individuals obtain income by doing exactly the same kind of work at the same time and place, the comparative amounts of income they obtain depend as a general rule, that is, taking the average of a large number of cases, on the comparative amounts of work they do. The more work one of them does in comparison with the others, the greater, of course, will be the value of his work compared with the value of theirs. In no actual society has it ever been true that the amounts earned by individuals doing the same kind of work are in every case exactly proportionate to the amount of work done. It could only be true in a society in which there existed no conservatism, not the slightest desire to go on doing something because it was the custom, and it is needless to say that such a society is an impossibility. Still, no one, or at all events no reasonable person, doubts that at present as a general rule the industrious earn larger incomes than the indolent in the same occupation, and that the strong and intelligent can if they choose earn more than the weak and unintelligent, in consequence of the fact that the industrious work longer or more continuously than the indolent, and that the strong and intelligent can do more work in a given time than the weak and unintelligent.

When several individuals do different kinds of work, the comparative amounts of income they obtain by it depend on the comparative value of the quantities of the different kinds of work which they do. If a man does work which is comparatively plentiful and lightly esteemed, he will earn less by a given amount of labour than a man who does work which is comparatively scarce and highly esteemed. The comparative plentifulness of different kinds of work obviously depends at any given time, or as long as the methods of production remain the same, on the comparative amounts of labour devoted to each kind of work, and, since co-operation by division of employments prevails, the amount of labour devoted to each kind of work depends on the comparative number of persons engaged in the different kinds of work, and the amount of labour each of them performs. Now a sudden reduction in the quantity of labour performed by the individuals engaged in any particular occupation, unaccompanied by a similar reduction in other occupations, will of course raise the comparative value of a given amount of the work they do; this is so well known that it constantly gives rise to what are called 'restrictions of production.' But a sudden reduction in the quantity of labour performed by the individuals engaged in any particular occupation, while it raises the comparative value of a given quantity of the produce of their labour, reduces at the same time the total quantity of the produce of their labour, and so may or may not raise their incomes in comparison with those obtained by other kinds of labour. For instance, if bootmakers throughout the world could and did agree to reduce their labour so that only nine pairs of boots should be made for every ten which would have been made in the absence of the agreement, they would not receive larger incomes unless the value of boots became so much greater that nine pairs of boots would be worth more than ten pairs would have been worth without the agreement. Thus the effect of 'working short time,' even supposing the whole of the individuals engaged in an occupation agree to it and perform their agreements, must always be difficult to forecast.

Consequently, at any given time the most direct, simple, and certain way of increasing or decreasing the remuneration of those engaged in any occupation in comparison with that of those engaged in other occupations, is to decrease or increase their number in comparison with the number of those engaged in other occupations. Remove half the bootmakers of the world, and the incomes of the remaining half will for a time be enormously greater than before; double the number of bootmakers, and the average income of bootmakers will be greatly less than before. The reason is that if the number of bootmakers is reduced, then either fewer boots will be made, and consequently the value of each pair will rise, or the reduced number of bootmakers will produce the same total number of boots as were produced before, or (as is more probable) fewer boots will be made altogether but more boots per head of bootmakers; obviously if the value of a pair of boots rises, or if more boots of the same value are made by each bootmaker, bootmakers' incomes must increase. We conclude, then, that at any given time the comparative amount of income which may be obtained by performing different kinds of labour, depends immediately on the comparative number of persons who are engaged in each occupation. Everyone knows that this is actually the case; what is called 'an increase of competition' in any particular trade usually means nothing more or less than an increase in the number of persons following that trade, and 'the state of the labour-market' only means the numbers of persons offering to do each kind of work.

Consequently if we wish to know what settles the comparative amounts of income individuals derive from different kinds of labour, we must answer the question, 'What settles the comparative numbers of persons engaged in the several occupations?'

The answer which has usually been made to this question is, 'Self-interest.' Now if self-interest alone settled the comparative numbers of persons engaged in the several occupations, we should expect that the advantages to be obtained by performing any one kind of labour would be equal to

those which could be obtained by performing any other kind of labour. That which, for want of a better name, we may call the whole advantageousness of all the different occupations would be equal; of course pecuniary earnings would not be the same in all trades, because in choosing an occupation a man is influenced by other considerations besides those which relate to pecuniary gain. He considers, for instance, 'the ease or hardship, the cleanliness or dirtiness, the honourableness or dishonourableness of the employment.' In the following passage Adam Smith describes admirably the state of things which, he thinks, would exist if the numbers of individuals engaged in different occupations were determined by self-interest alone:
'The whole of the advantages and disadvantages of the different employments of labour . . . must, in the same neighbourhood, be either perfectly equal or continually tending to equality. If in the same neighbourhood there was any employment evidently either more or less advantageous than the rest, so many people would crowd into it in the one case, and so many would desert it in the other, that its advantages would soon return to the level of other employments. This at least would be the case in a society where things were left to follow their natural course, where there was perfect liberty, and where every man was perfectly free both to choose what occupation he thought proper, and to change it as often as he thought proper. Every man's interest would prompt him to seek

the advantageous, and to shun the disadvantageous employment.'

But if we survey the field of employment we cannot fail to see that there are, as a matter of fact, enormous differences between the whole advantageousness of different employments. Everyone is aware that an average engine-driver is better off than an average dock-labourer, and that the whole advantageousness of labouring in many other trades and professions exceeds that of engine-driving. As it may be roughly put, the unskilled labourer is less well off than the skilled labourer, and the skilled labourer is less well off than the 'professional' or 'business' man, though there are many gradations in each of these three classes. Why do these differences exist? They are too lasting to be set down as temporary variations due to changes in the comparative estimation in which different satisfactions are held, or in the known means of producing those satisfactions; the effect of such alterations (supposing self-interest to regulate the comparative numbers engaged in the different occupations in the way described by Adam Smith) would soon be obliterated by readjustment of those numbers. Many people find it difficult to see that the existence of these differences of the advantageousness of occupations needs any explanation. If asked why mental and skilled labour are more advantageous than unskilled, they answer 'because the work done by mental and skilled labour is more useful,' or 'more socially important,' 'and therefore more valuable than work done by unskilled labour.' To this view there are two fatal objections: in the first place the more advantageous occupations are not more useful than the less advantageous, and in the second place, if they were more useful, that would not make the work done in them more valuable than that done in the other occupations. The labour of the highly-paid physician who cures a man of typhoid fever is not in the least more useful than the labour of the low-paid scavenger who prevents him having an attack of typhoid fever at all. A day's work of a navvy in stopping up some small leak in a dyke which protects millions of acres from inundation is immensely more useful, but not in the least more valuable, than a day's work of the same man when he is engaged in mending the bank of a duck-pond; the two day's work will each in ordinary circumstances exchange for a few shillings. The widespread opinion that the work done by those engaged in the more advantageous occupations is 'more useful and therefore more valuable' than that done by those engaged in the less advantageous occupations, is probably due merely to an ambiguity of the word 'valuable,' which is sometimes used in its economic sense already explained, and sometimes as merely equivalent to 'useful.' When, for instance, McCulloch calls the tenth chapter of the first book of the Wealth of Nations 'a valuable chapter,' he probably had not the slightest intention of suggesting that that chapter would exchange for several other chapters, or for more money than ordinary chapters; all he meant was that the chapter was useful and important. Now when 'valuable' means simply 'useful,' the more 'valuable' kinds of work are the more useful, but we are not to conclude from this that the more valuable kinds of work, in the economic sense of the word, are the more useful.

The differences of advantageousness which exist between various occupations are not due to any 'intrinsic' quality of the work done; they are simply due to the fact that the number of people engaged in some occupations is not large enough in comparison with the number engaged in other occupations in order to equalise the total advantageousness. If there were more people engaged in the occupations which are now comparatively highly paid and fewer in the other occupations, then the advantageousness of all occupations would be more nearly equal. What we want to know, then, is why self-interest does not lead to such a readjustment of the comparative numbers of people engaged in the various occupations as would make their advantageousness equal. Why, in short, do so many people do what Adam Smith says they will not do—choose the less advantageous occupation in preference to the more advantageous, and remain in the less advantageous occupation instead of changing to a more advantageous one?

First, let us consider changes of occupation. Why, when an occupation is found by those engaged in it to be a less advantageous occupation than some others, do not some of those engaged in it change to those other occupations, and so, by reducing the number engaged in the first occupation in comparison with the numbers engaged in the other occupations, bring its advantageousness up to a level with that of the other occupations? A tendency to this result is common enough. A fall of earnings in some one occupation compared with earnings in other occupations will almost always drive some people out of that occupation, though it will not usually drive out so many as to restore the old earnings. The reason why it will not drive out so many is that 'the most advantageous employment' is the employment which is most advantageous to those who have had experience in it, and not that which is most advantageous to a person altogether inexperienced in it. Consequently it is often, in spite of Adam Smith, a man's interest to remain in a less advantageous occupation instead of changing to a more advantageous one,—one which is more advantageous to workers experienced in it. For an ordinary adult navvy to set up as a dentist would be a very unprofitable change of occupation for him, however high the earnings of trained and experienced dentists might be compared with those of experienced navvies. For the most part it is each man's interest to keep to the employment to which he is accustomed, even if its advantages are much less than those obtained by people who are accustomed to other employments. Only within very narrow limits are changes of occupation ever likely to be profitable to ordinary men. It may often be a man's interest to change from one occupation to another which is very like it, it may sometimes be his interest to change from one occupation to another which has some resemblance to it, but it will scarcely ever be his interest to change from one occupation to a wholly different one. This fact will of course only account for temporary differences between the advantageousness of different employments, since the numbers of persons engaged in an occupation can be reduced in consequence of the places of those who die or retire in the ordinary course not being filled up, as surely, though not as quickly, as in consequence of some of those engaged in it leaving it and adopting some other occupation. But a 'temporary fluctuation' of earnings is not without importance. It may, indeed, as is often said, 'make no difference in the long run,' but individuals' lives do not last for 'the long run.' The short run, if the expression may be used, is often quite long enough to make the difference between a happy and a miserable life. If a man lives in a period which on the whole is a bad period for those engaged in his particular occupation, it is very little consolation to him to be told that the smallness of the advantageousness of that occupation is only temporary.

Secondly, let us consider the original choice of an occupation. Why, when young men and women are entering on working life, do they not always 'seek the advantageous and shun the disadvantageous employment,' so that, disregarding temporary fluctuations, the advantageousness of all occupations would be kept on a level? There are various reasons:—

(1.) The comparative advantageousness of different occupations is not always a matter of common knowledge. Some occupations are understocked owing to general ignorance of their advantages, and others are overstocked owing to general ignorance of their disadvantages. Differences of advantageousness arising from this cause, however, must always be trifling.

(2.) Legal freedom to adopt certain occupations and to avoid certain occupations does not exist. Many occupations, if adopted at all, must be adopted or prepared for by children when they are still legally under the control of their parents or other guardians. Many occupations are only practised by such children. No doubt going up chimneys was a 'disadvantageous employment'; why was it not 'shunned'? Obviously because those who adopted it had not 'perfect freedom to choose what occupation they thought proper.' There can be little doubt that some occupations are overstocked owing to the superior attractions which they present to the parents of children employed in them, and that others are understocked owing to the inferior attractions which they present to the parents. Parents are apt to put their sons and daughters into those occupations in which they will be able to 'get some good of them.'

(3.) Customs frequently hamper freedom to adopt certain occupations. One important reason why women as a rule earn so much less than men is that they are shut out by custom from many of the most advantageous occupations.

(4.) For the successful practice of many employments an expensive education or training is necessary. In most cases the cost of this must be defrayed by some one else than the person who is to profit by it; in the case of minors and others with property, the cost may be defrayed out of the property or the income derived from the property, and in some cases it can be defrayed by earnings made in another occupation, but these cases are the exception rather than the rule. The chief part of the cost of educating or training people for different employments is at present paid by the parents of the people educated or trained; the state, indeed, pays a very considerable proportion of the expense of general education, but this is rather preparation for all employments than for particular employments.

Now if parents could force children to repay out of their earnings whatever had been invested in special training for a particular employment, and if they could borrow on the security of this future repayment, then the training up of youth to particular occupations might become a matter conducted on strictly commercial principles. But the repayment by the trained worker of the cost incurred in training him, with its accrued interest, could not be enforced without the institution of slavery for those who refused to earn enough to pay the required amount; it is for this and other obvious reasons impossible for parents to borrow on the security of their children's future earnings. Consequently, as a matter of fact, whether a person is able or unable to adopt an occupation for which an expensive training is necessary, depends usually on the will and the power of his parents to pay the cost of the training for that occupation.

The largest actual differences of advantageousness which exist between various employments are due to this last cause. It is owing to the smallness of the number of parents who have both the power and the will to defray a large cost in training their children, that the advantageousness of those occupations which require an expensive training is always in excess of the advantageousness of other occupations. It is owing to the greatness of the number of parents who want either the power or the will to defray any cost at all for special training, that the sort of work which anyone not a complete idiot or invalid can do, is always miserably remunerated. When a person is one of the large number who have been in childhood badly nourished, badly housed, badly clothed, badly educated, and not at all trained to any particular occupation, let no one prate to him of his 'freedom to choose what occupation he thinks proper.' His legal freedom to choose many occupations is about as much use to him as his legal freedom to fly with wings in the air.

Economists have sometimes assumed that the advantageousness of the occupations for which an expensive training is necessary only exceeds that of the other occupations by an amount which exactly corresponds to the cost of the training. For example, if in one occupation an ordinary or average worker earns £300 a year, and in another occupation, equal to the first in respect of all advantages except pecuniary remuneration, an ordinary worker can only earn £100 a year, then the extra £200 a year would be considered simply repayment, so to speak, of the greater cost of preparation for that occupation with its accrued compound interest. There is, however, no real ground for this theory; it rests on a pure assumption. It is quite true, of course, that few parents will give their children an expensive training unless their children may reasonably be expected to get from that training some advantages over and above the advantages which will be obtained by those who have not received such a training. Few parents, for example, will spend an additional £100 on educating or training their son to some profession, unless the additional education or training thus obtained will eventually be at least as beneficial to the son as the £100 would have been if lent out or invested in some property. But because few parents will spend on preparing their children for an employment more than what is likely to be a remunerative investment, we are not to suppose that parents generally do or can spend so much. Common

§ 15. DETERMINATION OF LABOUR INCOMES. 97

observation shows us that as a matter of fact they do not spend so much. No one can doubt that the advantageousness of the employments for which expensive preparation is required is generally in excess of the advantageousness of those for which no expensive preparation is required, by much more than would correspond to the repayment of the extra cost with its accrued compound interest.

It must be noticed that even if the superior advantageousness of the higher forms of labour did form an exact compensation for the greater expense of preparing workers for them, this would not make all occupations equally advantageous. It is no disadvantage to a worker himself that his parents should have had to incur expenses for his training.

Before leaving this subject, it will be well to guard against a very common mistake by observing that in comparing the advantageousness of different occupations the length of the time for which labour is carried on in them must be considered. People are in the habit of comparing the pecuniary remuneration of different kinds of labour in several ways. Sometimes they consider a particular kind of labour highly paid if an average worker can earn much by an hour of it, sometimes if he can earn much by a day of it, sometimes if he can earn much in a week, sometimes if he can do so in a year. At the first glance we may be inclined to think that it makes no difference whether the earnings of an hour, a day, a week, or a year be taken for the purpose of comparison. If a man can

H

earn much by a particular form of labour in an hour, surely he can do so in any other period of time. This, however, is by no means the case. The number of hours in a day's work is not the same in all occupations, nor is the number of days in a week's work, nor the number of weeks in a year's work. Consequently an occupation in which much can be earned in one of the periods is not necessarily an occupation in which much can be earned in the other periods. What period of time are we then to take, when we wish to compare the advantageousness of different occupations? The best plan is to take the amount of money which can be earned by the average worker in a particular occupation in an average lifetime as the advantage of that occupation represented by pecuniary remuneration, and then to reckon the length of the actual labour time in the lifetime as a disadvantage, or (which is the same thing) to reckon the length of the leisure time as an advantage. The time spent in preparing for the occupation must be included in the labour time. How great an advantage leisure time will be considered depends on many circumstances. It depends largely on the amount of income obtained in the occupation. A person who obtains a large income will naturally forego a larger proportion of it for the sake of any given increase of leisure time than a person who obtains a small income. So an occupation in which average earnings are £50 and working time 300 days a year, will be considered in all probability more advantageous than an occupation (similar in all other respects) in which average earnings are £48 and working time 264 days a year. But an occupation in which average earnings are £500 and working time 300 days will probably be considered less advantageous than an occupation (similar in all other respects) in which average earnings are £480 and working time 264 days a year. When leisure time comes at irregular intervals and is of uncertain duration it is not of much use, and when a man obtains it only by being 'out of work' the advantage of it is counter-balanced by the disadvantage of anxiety.

§ 16. Causes which determine the Comparative Size of the Incomes individuals derive from Property.

Having considered the causes of differences of earnings, we now proceed to the consideration of the causes of differences of income derived from property. These causes are evidently identical with those which determine how much property each man has.

The world as a whole adds to its property or stock of useful material objects only by saving, that is by consuming, using up, wearing out and allowing to fall into decay less than it produces. Saving is one way, though not the only way, by which individuals obtain property. How much a person saves depends partly on his temperament and partly on the amount of his income. An economical person often saves a considerable amount out of £500 a year; an extravagant person often saves nothing out of £50,000 a year. But it evidently requires a vastly greater amount of self-control to save £10 out of £50 a year than to save £10,000 or even £40,000 out of £50,000 a year.

It must be noticed here that property cannot be amassed 'by speculation,' unless the speculation be accompanied by saving. What a man gains by speculation is in the first instance income to him; it is income obtained by means of the possession of property. There is no reason why a man should not make an income by buying and selling land or stocks and shares as well as by buying and selling tea and sugar. No doubt the gains of speculation are often very great in proportion to the value of the property, but so are the losses, and however great the gains may be they are still income. Now if a man spends all the income which he derives from speculation he will obviously amass no property by means of his speculations.

If saving were the only means by which individuals could obtain property and income derived from property, colossal fortunes would be almost unknown, and very large fortunes would be much rarer than they are. Everyone would have to begin with no property, and so the nucleus of every man's savings would have to be amounts saved from the earnings of his labour. Thus none except those whose genius enabled them to earn extraordinary amounts, would be able in the

§ 16. DETERMINATION OF PROPERTY INCOMES.

limits of their lifetime to save enough to amass a very great quantity of property. There are, however, several lawful methods besides saving by which an individual can acquire property. He may acquire it by gift from another individual or from the State, by prescription, or by bequest or inheritance. The amount of property acquired by gift from individuals or by grant from the State is not very large. Individuals acquired a considerable amount of property by prescription when the gradual change from common to separate cultivation of land was proceeding, but in these days few are allowed to remain undisturbed in the possession of what does not belong to them long enough for it to become their property by prescription. A much larger portion of existing property has come into the hands of its present owners by way of inheritance and bequest. Anyone can see that property in land is handed down from generation to generation, but the fact that most other property is subject to frequent renewal is sometimes allowed to obscure the plain fact that all kinds of property are handed down from generation to generation in just the same way as land. He who inherits or receives as a legacy a thousand pounds' worth of some kind of property which has to be renewed once a month, is just as much benefited by the inheritance or legacy as he who inherits a thousand pounds' worth of land.

Over and above the portion of existing property

which has come into its present owners' hands directly owing to bequest and inheritance, there is another portion which has come into their hands indirectly owing to bequest and inheritance. This is that amount of the savings of the present owners of property which is due to their having had incomes derived from property obtained by bequest and inheritance to save out of. Directly and indirectly far the greater portion of existing property in this country has come into its present owners' possession owing to bequest and inheritance.

We must consequently conclude that the comparative amounts of income men derive from the possession of property are generally still more dependent on the wealth of their parents than the amounts of income which they earn by labour.

§ 17. Causes which determine the Comparative Size of the Income derived from Property and the Income derived from Labour.

When we have considered separately, first, the causes which settle the comparative amounts of income individuals derive from labour, and, secondly, the causes which settle the comparative amounts of income individuals derive from property, we have still to consider the causes which make Property, or proprietors as such, well or ill off compared with Labour, or labourers as such.

In many discussions as to the interests of Property and Labour, confusion results from a want of recognition of the fact that those interests may be, and commonly are, compared in two wholly different ways. Sometimes Property is considered better off compared with Labour when the income which can be derived from saving a hundred days' earnings is equal to many days' earnings, than when it is equal only to a few days' earnings. Sometimes, on the other hand, Property is considered better off compared with Labour when the whole income derived from all existing property is large compared with the whole income derived from labour, than when it is small compared with that quantity.

By the first of the two methods of comparing the position of Property and Labour as regards income, Property is considered the better off in comparison with Labour the higher the rate of interest may be. If an income equal to ten days' earnings can be annually derived from the possession of property representing a hundred days' earnings, we say that the rate of interest is ten per cent. per annum; if income equal only to five days' earnings can be derived from such property, we say that the rate of interest is five per cent. per annum. The rate of interest is nothing but the proportion which exists between the value of property itself and the value of the use of it for a given period of time. Five per cent. per annum is, of course, if paid monthly, just the same thing as a penny per pound per month; there is no peculiar virtue in the number one hundred, or in the period of time during which the earth revolves round the sun. It is customary in England at the present time to reckon interest as so much per hundred per year, but it has been customary at other times and places to reckon it by the use of other numbers and periods of time.

Now what is meant by the highness or lowness of 'the rate of interest' at any given time? Are there not many rates of interest—many ratios between the value of property and the value of the use of it—prevailing at the same time? It is sometimes asserted, with greater boldness than accuracy, that the rate of interest is uniform at any given time. This is not quite true; it is true indeed that the rough-and-ready general rule is that the income derived from different properties varies with their value. If A has property worth £100,000 and B property worth only £10,000, we certainly expect to find that A has a larger income from his property than B. So, too, if C has an income of £1,000 a year from his property, we should expect him to have property worth more than that of D, who obtains only £500 a year from his property. But we should not be in the least surprised to find that A's income was not exactly ten times the size of B's, or that C's property was not worth exactly double what B's was worth. At the same time and place the rate of interest is higher in the case of investments supposed to be insecure than in the case of investments supposed to be secure. It is so very much more pleasant to feel assured of an income than to feel dubious on the subject, that it would be absurd to expect the ratio between the value of the property and the value of a year's use of it to be the same where the income is secure as where it is insecure. The anxiety of mind undergone by the owner of the insecure property has to be paid for by a larger income; no one would be willing to undergo the anxiety of possessing insecure property, if only the same income could be derived from a given amount of it as from the same amount of secure property. It is said by those who maintain the doctrine of a uniform rate of interest that 'in the long run,' or taking very large amounts of property at once, the holders of insecure property receive the same income as the holders of an equal amount of secure property. It is certainly very probable that, owing to their losses, they do not receive more than the owners of secure property, but it is quite possible that they may receive less. There is nothing to show that the compensation for anxiety of mind is exactly so great as to equalise all investments in the long run; where a gambling spirit prevails the compensation will be insufficient, and where a 'want of enterprise' or over-caution prevails it will be more than sufficient. Even at the same time and place different individuals estimate risk very differently, and there is no reason to suppose that the average estimate is exactly correct, although it may be nearly so. Probably on the whole risks are under-estimated, so that the more secure investments are the best in the long run, but this is by no means certain. Granting, however, for the purposes of argument, that, after deducting losses, equal amounts of income are in the long run derived from equal amounts of property, this would not make the rate of interest uniform. If we want to know what is the average rate of interest obtained by the proprietors of banks, must we reckon in all the extinct broken banks as well as the existing banks? When we speak of the rate of interest obtained by owning any particular kind of property, we mean the rate actually obtained without deduction for losses, and everyone consequently in ordinary life recognises the co-existence of different rates of interest due to differences of security. Even where the security is considered to be exactly the same, there may be more than one rate of interest, owing to several causes, the most important of which, perhaps, is that it is more convenient to own property which can be easily sold than property which cannot. People are willing to pay something for this convenience, and so the rate of interest is lower in the case of property which is easy to sell than in the case of property which takes time to sell. It is a well-known fact on the Stock Exchange that, owing to this reason, stocks of which a large quantity exists are more highly priced than exactly similar stocks of which there is only a small quantity.

The co-existence of a number, an immense number, of different rates of interest does not make it impossible to speak intelligibly of the highness or lowness of the rate of interest in general. It makes it impossible to say that the rate of interest at such and such a time is so much per cent., but it does not make it impossible to say that the rate of interest generally has increased or decreased. There are causes which affect the whole of the particular rates of interest, making them rise or fall together, and when we speak of a rise or fall in the general rate of interest we mean that some of these causes have been at work. Whether the general rate of interest is higher or lower at one time or place than at another, may be discovered by comparing the rate of interest obtained on what are considered the very safest investments at the two times or places. The other rates are sure to vary along with this rate exactly enough for all practical purposes.

Admitting, then, that in spite of the existence of different rates of interest at one and the same time we may yet speak of the general rate of interest as high or low, let us consider what the highness or lowness of that rate depends upon. It depends immediately upon, or rather it is identical with, the ratio between the amount which can be added directly to the income of the community by a given amount of additional labour and the amount which can be added to the income of each future year by saving the produce of that amount of labour, that is, by adding it to the existing stock of useful material objects. If a community produces an income of

£5,000,000 a day, and the rate of interest be taken to be four per cent., then a day's income saved would obviously mean a future increase of annual income amounting to £200,000; if the rate of interest were twenty per cent., the saving of a day's income would mean a future increase of annual income amounting to £1,000,000. Now whether the saving of £5,000,000 will bring in future income to the amount of £200,000 or £1,000,000 clearly depends on the amount of unused methods which are known of saving future labour by the expenditure of present labour. If no way is known of expending one day's labour in such a way as to save more than one twenty-fifth of a day's labour in future years, interest will be only four per cent.; if some one discovers a way of expending one day's labour so as to save one-fifth of a day's labour in future years, interest will rise to twenty per cent., but will fall again as this method of saving labour is taken advantage of. Discoveries of new ways of making savings profitable are favourable to a rise of the rate of interest, and increases of the stock of existing property are favourable to a fall of the rate of interest. Whether the rate actually rises or falls depends on the comparative strength of these two opposing forces.

The richer as regards income a community grows, the less likely is the progress of invention to be able to counteract the influence of additions to the stock of existing property upon the rate of interest. This is the consequence of the fact that it is much easier for a rich people to save than for a poor one. A man who is very nearly starved will require, in order to induce him to save, a much higher rate of interest than a millionaire; obviously the offer of a thousand per cent. per annum would not induce a starving man to lend his last penny instead of buying food with it. Similarly, a poor community, a community in which the average income is low, will not be induced to save except by a rate which would seem enormous to a rich community; immediate satisfactions will be more desired by the poor community in comparison with future ones than they will be by the rich community.

By the second of the two methods of comparing the position of Property and Labour as regards income, Property is considered well or ill off in comparison with Labour according as the whole income derived from all existing property is great or small compared with the whole income derived from every kind of labour.

One of the worst mistakes which can be made in political economy is to confuse the two methods of comparing the position of Property and Labour, to suppose, in short, either that the rate of interest is the ratio which property's total income bears to labour's total income, or that the highness or lowness of the rate of interest indicates that the income of Property is high or low compared with that of Labour. To suppose that the rate of interest is identical with the ratio between the total incomes of Property and Labour is too childish an error to need refutation. Because the rate of interest is, say, four per cent., we are not to conclude that four per cent. of the total income of the community goes to Property and the remaining ninety-six per cent. to Labour, any more than we are to conclude that if the owner of a factory receives, as owner, five per cent. on his property, then the workers as such receive ninety-five per cent. of the produce of the factory. Clearly the rate of interest and the ratio between the incomes of Property and Labour would only be identical if the total income and the total property were of exactly the same value. If, for instance, the total property of a community were worth a thousand million pounds and the total income amounted to the same sum, then, if the rate of interest were four per cent., Property's total income would really be to Labour's as four is to one hundred.

To suppose that Property's total income is necessarily high in proportion to Labour's when the rate of interest is high, and low when the rate of interest is low, is of course the same error in a slightly less definite form. Only if some fixed ratio existed between the value of the whole existing property and the value of the whole income, would the proportion between the income of property and that of labour necessarily vary with the rate of interest. Suppose, for instance, that the total income of a community was always one-tenth of the value of the total property, then a four per cent. rate of interest would give Property four-tenths of the total income, a three per cent. rate of interest would give Property three-tenths, and so on; if the total income was always one-eighth of the value of the total property four per cent. would give Property $\frac{32}{100}$, and three per cent. would give it $\frac{24}{100}$, and so on. As a matter of fact, of course, the ratio between the value of the stock of property and the value of the total income varies, so that the rate of interest by itself tells us nothing about the ratio between the total income of Property and the total income of Labour. A five per cent. rate of interest would give Property half the total income where the value of the whole stock of property was ten times as great as that of the total income; the same rate of interest would only give Property a quarter of the total income where the value of the whole property was only five times as great as that of the total income.

We should only fall into another error if we were to suppose that the rate of interest and the ratio between the total income of a community and the value of its total property jointly settled the proportion which Property's income bears to Labour's. They indicate it, but they no more settle it than the mercury in the thermometer settles the temperature.

The question, 'What is the proportion between the total income of Property and the total income of Labour?' is simply synonymous with the question, 'What is the proportion between the total value of the use of all existing property for a given period of time and the total value of all work performed in the same period of time?' The comparative value of these two collections of commodities is settled in just the same way as the comparative value of any other two collections of commodities; the value of each commodity in the collections is settled by its comparative plentifulness and the comparative estimation in which it is held, and the value of the whole collections is discovered by adding together the value of all the different commodities of which they are composed. No special rules can be laid down for this particular case of value. Inventions may help to increase or to decrease Property's proportion of the total income; the invention of locomotives was probably favourable to Property's proportion, and the invention of the telegraph has almost certainly been unfavourable to it. An increase of the total amount of property, unaccompanied by an increase of the total amount of labour performed, would tend to lower the value of the use of some of the units of the property taken separately; but, on the other hand, it would increase the number of those units taken together. An increase of the labour performed, or, as we may put it roughly, an increase of the population, would tend to lower the value of some of the units, so to speak, of work done; but, on the other hand, it would increase the number of those units taken together. Consequently it is impossible to say that relative increases or decreases of property or population will always affect in the same way the comparative value of the use of the whole of the property and of the work done. Political Economy can lay down no more rules about the comparative value of these two collections of commodities than it can lay down respecting the comparative value of the total oat-crop and the total wheat-crop. Some historical generalisations might perhaps be deduced from statistics showing the actual amount of the two incomes at various times in real societies, but the requisite statistics are not obtainable.

This fact is not one over which much regret need be felt, since it is of no practical interest to any human being whether the income of Property bears a large or small proportion to that of Labour: 'Labour' and 'Property' are not themselves human beings nor do they even represent classes of human beings. There never has been, and there never will be, a society of free men consisting only of pure proprietors who own property and do no work, on the one hand, and pure labourers who work and own no property on the other. There may be, it is true, societies like that which exists in this country at present, in which there are millions of human beings who own absolutely no property; such are children and others supported entirely by their relations or friends, indoor paupers, prisoners and bankrupts. But it is certainly not of these that people think when they talk of a class of 'Labourers.' Nearly all independent adults in every civilised country both own some property and do some work, and are therefore both proprietors and labourers. Moreover a considerable number of these proprietor-labourers receive about half their income from property and the other half from labour, and are consequently as much proprietors as they are labourers.

But even if societies were divided sharply into two classes, one consisting of pure proprietors and the other of pure labourers, it would not necessarily follow that individual labourers would be any better off in comparison with individual proprietors in consequence of a rise in the proportion borne by Labour's total income to that of Property, or that they would be any worse off in comparison with individual proprietors in consequence of a fall in that proportion. Let us imagine a very small community consisting of 12 proprietors with a total income of £2,400, and 120 labourers with a total income of £4,800. Here the total income of Property is half that of Labour, but the average proprietor's income, £200, is to the average labourer's income, £40, as five is to one. Now supposing that in the course of time we find that the total income of Labour has increased to £14,400 and the total income of Property only to £4,800, so that Labour's total income has become three times as large as that of Property instead of only twice as large, will this by itself prove that individual labourers are now better off in comparison with individual proprietors than before? By no means, since the number of labourers may have risen, say,

§ 17. PROPERTY AND LABOUR. 115

from 120 to 480, while the number of proprietors may have risen only from 12 to 16, so that the average proprietor will now have £300 a year instead of £200 and the average labourer £30 instead of £40, that is to say, the average proprietor will be ten times as rich as the average labourer instead of only five times as rich. Conversely, if the total income of Labour had increased from £4,800 only to £7,200, while the total income of Property had increased from £1,200 to £6,000, so that Property's income had become equal to five-sixths of that of Labour instead of one half, would this by itself prove that the average labourer had become worse off in comparison with the average proprietor than before? No; for the number of proprietors might have increased to 40 while the number of labourers had only increased to 144, so that the average proprietor would have £150 a year instead of £200 and the average labourer £50 instead of £40, that is to say, the average proprietor would be only three times as rich as the average labourer instead of five times as rich.

PART III.

THE PROMOTION OF MATERIAL WELFARE BY THE STATE.

§ 1. CHARACTER OF THE CO-OPERATION INVOLVED IN STATE EFFORT AFTER WEALTH.

Individualistic effort working by means of private property and exchange of commodities does not at present provide the whole of the material welfare enjoyed by the inhabitants of civilised countries. Besides individualistic effort there is another agency for the promotion of material welfare, the State. For economic purposes the State may be considered as an association or corporation which consists at any given time of the whole of the inhabitants of a certain territory. Under the imperial authority there exist corporations or associations of the whole of the inhabitants of smaller areas, such as counties, cities, and sanitary districts, which must not be forgotten in treating of the State and its action. The character of the association represented by the State is peculiar. The association is not exactly a voluntary association, since individuals are born members of it and

§ 1.   STATE CO-OPERATION. 117

subject to its rules or laws. On the other hand it is not fair to describe it as a compulsory association continually engaged in the coercion of unwilling members. The coercive power of governments is commonly enormously over-rated. There is a very true proverb that one man can take a horse to the water, but ten cannot make him drink. The government of a state may make what laws it pleases, but it depends on the will of its subjects whether they will be carried out or not. Even where the government represents the majority of the inhabitants of a country, it must always fail in coercing any considerable minority, if that minority is strongly determined not to obey. Ten million men no doubt will in all probability vanquish one million men in battle, and be able if they choose either to nearly exterminate them or to drive them away, but they will never be able to bear the expense of keeping them all in prison or in chains. Against determined passive resistance the strongest government strikes its head in vain. The business of a State is generally carried on by means of mutual forbearance. Each man gets his own way on some points, and has to sacrifice his wishes on others. There are few more groundless assumptions than the common one that in democratic countries, where the principle that questions are to be decided by the majority of votes is accepted, one particular set of individuals called 'the majority' is perpetually tyrannising over another set of individuals called 'the minority.' The fact is, of course, that the majority on one subject is not composed of the same persons as the majority on other subjects; very few men are in the minority on every subject of political interest. It is true that where party government prevails, one party may be in power for a long time, and also that parties generally consist, as regards the bulk of their members, of the same persons from year to year. But, as everyone knows, 'a united party' is a figment of the imagination of the political partisan; no party is united, and in most parties there is nearly as much divergence of opinion as there is in the nation which is divided into parties. Consequently, it by no means follows that because the party to which a man prefers on the whole to attach himself is in power, therefore he is getting his own way on all the political questions which arise.

What really distinguishes the association represented by the State from other associations is its territorial basis. If it were not necessarily established on a territorial basis it might be a purely voluntary association. As it is, anyone may practically cease to be a member of it, and cease to be subject to its laws in person and property, by simply removing himself and his property from the territory over which it claims authority. Thus the association is only a degree more compulsory in character than the relation between a tenant and his landlord. It is true that a man who has left the dominions of the state to which he originally belonged does not technically cease to be a subject of that state till he has gone through certain formalities, but this fact is of very small practical importance. Except in some special cases, men live under the laws of the state in whose territory they are domiciled, pay its taxes, and enjoy nearly all the benefits it confers, and it really makes little difference to them whether they are technically subjects of some other state or not.

That there should be an authority possessing jurisdiction over every person and thing existing on a given territory is an absolute necessity for the maintenance of any kind of civilised and settled society. Without such an authority it would be impossible for individualistic effort to be carried on. Individuals would not be able to work for their own benefit in peace, and private property could not be effectively protected in the absence of an organisation for defence against evil doers and well defined rules as to what constitutes evil doing. The foundation of associations for mutual protection on some other basis than a territorial one could only lead to continual faction fights.

Besides the elementary and necessary functions of preserving the public peace and deciding what constitutes private property, modern states perform various other functions. They not only give individualistic effort a free field for the production of wealth, but also enable the united effort of their subjects to produce various kinds of wealth directly.

There is no reason why the review of this part of the action of the State should be, as it often is, obscured by prejudices arising from the adoption of particular theories of progress. Each man may have his own Utopia, provided that he expects its realisation only in a somewhat remote future, as the eventual result of gradual changes, each of which will be in its time neither immoral nor inexpedient. It is quite possible that in the distant future such changes will take place as will lead either to the entire disappearance of State property and State action in economic matters, or to the entire disappearance of private property and individualistic effort after wealth. Meantime no reasonable man can doubt that if either State action or individualistic action is destined to disappear, it will do so in such a slow and gradual manner that the process will be, to the ordinary intelligence, imperceptible. For the present, and for at any rate a considerable time to come, both State action and individualistic action are and will be absolutely necessary, and the cause of progress, whatever be its goal, will not be in the least advanced by attempts to establish a rule that the one is always productive of good results and the other always productive of bad results.

But while we condemn indiscriminate attacks upon all kinds of State action we must be careful not to fall into another error, that of supposing that a state cannot adopt a course of action extremely pernicious to the general material welfare. An instance of such a course of action is the adoption of the policy known as Protection.

§ 2. PROTECTION.

The policy which is known as Protection consists in preventing or hampering the competition of foreigners with the subjects of the State adopting a Protective policy. It is usually carried out either by prohibiting altogether or by hampering in some way the importation of a kind of commodity which can be produced within the country and the production of which within the country is not subject to a corresponding restriction. The hampering of the importation of the kind of commodity in question is most commonly accomplished by levying a tax—a customs duty—from the importers of that kind of commodity. There are arguments which may be held to justify Protection in particular cases. Protection may, for instance, be necessary in some cases for national security, and it is possible though not probable that temporary Protection may in some cases be in the long run advantageous to a country by enabling particular kinds of industry to be set on foot in it.

But as a rule Protection is established and maintained in consequence of complete misconceptions as to what constitutes the advantage of foreign trade.

The oldest and crudest of these misconceptions is that foreign trade is beneficial to a nation only when the value of the exports exceeds the value of the imports. Those who hold this view think that the difference between the price of the imports and that of the exports must be paid in money, and therefore a nation whose 'exports exceed her imports' must be growing richer, and a nation whose 'imports exceed her exports' must be growing poorer. The refutation of this theory is of course easy enough. In the first place, in the actual cases when the exports exceed the imports, or the imports exceed the exports, statistics show that the difference is not as a matter of fact paid in money; for instance, the value of the imports into this country has long so enormously exceeded that of the exports that if the difference had been paid in gold, the last sovereign would long ago have left our shores. In the second place, supposing that the difference between the value of the imports and that of the exports did represent the import or the export of so much gold, it does not follow that the countries whose exports exceeded their imports would be growing richer, and that those whose imports exceeded their exports would be growing poorer. A large stock of gold is worth no more than an equally valuable stock of any other commodity, and a perpetual importation of gold is no more a sign of growing wealth than the perpetual importation of any other metal. It is impossible that a country could be so drained of its cash by foreign commerce that it would not be able to carry on its internal commerce, for the obvious reason that if coin began to get scarce in the country, its value in all other commodities would rise within the country, that is to say 'prices' would fall, and it would become more profitable to buy some commodities within the country than to go on buying them abroad, so that importation would be checked and exportation encouraged till the drain of cash came to an end.

Granting that the difference between imports and exports does not, as is evident, represent gold or silver payments, some protectionists occasionally advance the proposition that it represents debts which the country is contracting or else property within the country which is passing into the hands of foreigners. This is no doubt sometimes partially, at any rate, the case. But the subject cannot possibly be understood unless we remember that the published value of both imports and exports is their value when they cross the frontier of the country. Generally speaking, therefore, exports have still to be carried a long distance, and imports only a short distance, after their value is set down. The consequence is that though the total imports of all the countries of the world taken together are obviously the same thing as the total exports, the value of the total imports greatly exceeds that of the exports. The difference is the cost of conveyance, and is received, in goods, by the countries whose men and ships do the work of conveyance. Further differences between the values of imports and exports are to be accounted for by the fact that the individuals who compose one nation may receive more income from investments abroad than foreigners receive from investments within the territory of that nation, and the individuals who compose another nation may receive less income from investments in foreign countries than foreigners receive from investments within the territory of that nation. The difference between the income due to foreigners and the income due from them must of course be paid in commodities of some kind, so that when the income due to foreigners exceeds that due from foreigners, exports must be made for which no imports are received in exchange, and *vice versa*. When, however, the investments are being made, the case is in a sense reversed. The country which is making the largest foreign investments will have to make exports for which no imports are received in exchange, and the country in which the greatest foreign investments are being made will receive imports for which it has sent abroad no exports.

The second and more modern of the great misconceptions on which Protection is commonly based is that the advantage of foreign trade to a nation consists in its 'giving employment' to the producers of the exports. Now in the first place, as we saw at the outset of our inquiry, there can never be too little work for men to do, so that even supposing foreigners were kind enough to send the imports as a free gift, there is no reason to suppose that a cessation of exports would lead to a permanent 'want of work.' In the second place, a cessation

§ 2. PROTECTION.

of exports usually means a cessation of imports, so that those who were formerly engaged in producing the exports would, when the exports ceased, probably be able to find employment in producing the commodities which used to be imported. Much alarm need not be felt at every petty loss of export trade. The cause of the cessation of the export of any particular commodity generally is that the producers no longer receive as great remuneration as they can obtain in some other branch of production. This may be the case either owing to a decrease in the remuneration obtained by producing that commodity, or owing to an increase in the remuneration obtainable in other trades. If the cessation of a particular export is due to the second of these causes, it is a sign of prosperity.

Having now considered the grounds on which Protection commonly rests, let us proceed to examine its ordinary effects on the general material welfare.

The effect of a protective duty upon an article actually imported into a country in considerable quantities must evidently be in the first place to decrease the profits of the importers, and consequently to check importation. This restriction on the supply of the commodity will raise its value within the country; for a time the gains of the home producers will be increased. Soon their extraordinary gains will attract new men into the trade, and the production of the commodity will be increased. The value of the commodity must then fall to a point which will reduce the gains of the home producers to their ordinary level. The value of the commodity will not generally fall to the level at which it stood before the imposition of the duty. To produce the additional quantity of the commodity within the country will take a more than proportionate addition to the labour expended in producing it, and this has to be paid for in an increase of the price of the commodity. All the extra labour paid for in the increase of the price of the commodity is simply thrown away by the act of the State in imposing the protective duty; this is the measure of the loss to the whole community. Over and above this loss to the whole community, the consumers or users of the commodity have to pay the duty itself, if any part of the commodity continues to be imported, and frequently another sum to some class of persons who, taken collectively, have a monopoly of the instruments of production used in producing the commodity within the country.

These facts may be made more clear by means of a concrete example.

At present this country, or to speak more literally, individuals who inhabit this country, export large quantities of manufactured articles and import large quantities of food. That is to say, they exchange manufactures for food. If a protective duty were now imposed on the importation of food, what would be the result? In the first place there would evidently be a rise in the price of food, for the import duty would necessarily have the effect of restricting the supply from abroad, and thus reducing the whole supply. The rise in the price would have the temporary effect of increasing the incomes of the actual home producers of food, such as farmers and agricultural labourers; it would also have the temporary effect of decreasing the material welfare of all other classes, since these would all have to pay more (give more of their productions in exchange) for their food than before. In time, probably in a short time, competition would reduce the agricultural class and the other classes to their old relative position, since the great gains of the agricultural class would lead to more labour being employed in agriculture and less in other kinds of industries, and this, of course, would soon reduce the value of agricultural produce in proportion to the value of other produce. By this diversion of labour from manufacturing to agricultural industry the owners of such instruments of production as coal mines would obviously be injured, and the owners of such instruments as agricultural land would obviously be benefited. The whole community taken together would suffer a loss because its labour would now be less productive than before. 'Why should it be less productive?' asks the Protectionist. Because it is easier for the inhabitants of this country to obtain a large proportion of their food by manufacturing articles which they give in exchange for food than to obtain the whole of their food by producing it within the country. 'How do we know that it is easier?' We know that it is easier because if it were not easier there would be at present, under free trade, more agricultural and less manufacturing industry than there is. There is no explanation of the historical increase of manufacturing industry relatively to agricultural industry in this country except that millions of individuals have found it more easy to make a living by engaging in manufacturing than by engaging in agricultural industry.

The real economic advantage of international trade is that it makes it possible to localise industries in the places best suited for carrying them on. The countries which derive most benefit from international trade are those which are least fitted for carrying on all kinds of industries, and the countries which derive least benefit from it are those which are most fitted for carrying on all kinds of industries. Thus a country which contains many climates, soils, and minerals, may with almost complete impunity put hindrances in the way of its foreign trade which would be fatal to the prosperity of a country which contains but one climate, few soils, and few or no minerals. Speaking roughly then, we may say that the larger a country is, the less is the importance of its foreign trade to it. The importance of international trade between large countries is usually immensely exaggerated. This exaggeration is probably due to the publication of the statistics of foreign trade.

If we could have a statement of the value of the imports and exports of each county in the United Kingdom put before us every year, we should think less of the imports and exports of the whole country.

The fact that the importance of international trade is exaggerated of course forms no justification for hampering it.

§ 3. THE SALE OF COMMODITIES BY THE STATE.

The benefits which the inhabitants of a country like our own provide for themselves by united effort through the organisation of the State may for economic purposes be conveniently divided into two classes:—

1. Commodities which the State, including 'local authorities,' acting much in the same way as a private individual, sells to purchasers.

2. Benefits which the State confers on the general public or on particular individuals or classes gratuitously, that is to say, without taking in exchange from those who receive the benefits a payment proportionate to the amount of benefit received in each case.

In this section we will deal only with the first class, the commodities sold by the State.

The great agency through which the State in this country sells commodities is the Post Office. The Post Office sells the commodities involved in the carriage of letters and of small parcels, and the transmission of telegrams. It takes charge of small sums of money, exacting as its remuneration the difference between the interest it receives for the wealth so placed in its hands and the interest it pays to the depositors. It also facilitates the transmission of small sums from place to place by means of postal and money orders. Besides these commodities, the imperial government also sells the use of the crown lands, and local governments often sell various commodities, the most important of which are gas and water, the use of bridges, docks, and piers. In some countries the State undertakes the much larger business of carrying passengers and goods by railway.

To be properly remunerative to the State, as to a private individual, the price at which a commodity is sold must be sufficient to pay interest on the capital invested in the business, that is to say, to pay for the use of the property which must be used in producing the commodity, as well as to pay the more immediate cost of its production in wages and materials. There is no ground at all for the theory sometimes put forward that the State should deliberately abstain from making a profit from the working of an institution like the Post Office. Taxpayers are indeed nearly all users of the Post Office, and users of the Post Office are nearly all taxpayers, but there is nothing to show that people are taxed in the same proportions as they use the Post Office—the largest taxpayers are not necessarily the largest users of the Post Office. Con-

§ 3. SALE OF COMMODITIES BY THE STATE.

sequently it is not a matter of complete indifference whether the State, which in this case means the taxpayers, makes a profit on the business or not. The only question difficult to decide is how much interest on the capital invested the State ought to obtain, in order to make the business remunerative but not a source of taxation. When the State has no monopoly, or only a monopoly secured by driving out all competitors in fair commercial rivalry (if such a case has ever occurred), it may charge what it can get for the commodity sold without making the business a source of taxation. But when the State has conferred on itself a monopoly of a business, it is evident that to charge the price which would bring in the largest profit would often be simply equivalent to laying a tax on the commodity. In this case the price charged should only be such as would produce a rate of interest which would satisfy private individuals or joint-stock companies, supposing there were no monopoly. The rate of interest should be reckoned in relation to the actual market value of the property used, not in relation to what it may have originally cost the State. When the State makes a bad investment the loss should be written off once for all as soon as it is discovered. If, for instance, a State has bought telegraph apparatus for far more than it is worth, there can be no reason why the senders of telegrams, and not the whole body of taxpayers, should pay for the mistake.

Much too great importance is commonly attributed to this part of State-action, the sale of commodities. We may be sure that if the State had not happened to undertake the business of carrying letters some private organisation would have been established for the purpose; whether it would have done the work better or worse than the present State Post Office does it, is a question which we have no means of answering. So too on the other hand, if the State in this country had undertaken the provision of railways, we should have had a railway system of some sort; it might have been a better or it might have been a worse system; whether it would have been better or worse would have depended on the wisdom of those who had the largest share in devising and extending it, and who these persons would have been, and what their wisdom would have been, we have no means of telling. It is quite useless to attempt to decide such questions by the aid of general principles. The only reliable general principle bearing on the matter is that good private management is superior to bad State management, and that good State management is superior to bad private management. There is really no reason to suppose that, where public criticism is possible and freely allowed, State management is on the average either better or worse than the management of large joint-stock businesses.

We may conclude that the sale of commodities by the State, when the commodities are sold at their market price, has no very important effect on the welfare of the nation in general. That it has no effect on the relative size of individuals' incomes is evident enough. He who receives much benefit from the State in this way pays much, and he who receives little pays little; the proportions existing between incomes are left wholly undisturbed. If, however, the State sells any commodities for less than a remunerative price, it confers a bounty, and if, on the other hand, it takes advantage of a legal monopoly which it has conferred on itself and sells any commodities at more than their market price, it imposes a tax.

§ 4. THE GRATUITOUS PROVISION OF BENEFITS BY THE STATE.

Far more important in its effects on general and particular material welfare than the sale of commodities by the State, is the gratuitous provision of benefits by the State. Such benefits are more or less complete protection from assault, robbery, and fraud, the freedom of locomotion and transport which results from State-maintenance of roads and streets and State regulation of water traffic, drainage and other sanitary provisions, public parks, elementary education, maintenance of those who cannot or will not maintain themselves and who are not maintained by friends or charitable institutions. The good or bad effect of the provision of these gratuitous benefits on the general welfare is not capable of being conclusively demonstrated. Those who disbelieve in the efficacy of State action in promoting material welfare can easily draw charming pictures of the way in which, as they imagine, private enterprise would have supplied the various benefits if the State had never 'interfered,' and there is no way of proving whether such pictures would have been realised or not. The great preponderance of opinion, it need scarcely be said, is in favour of the State. Those who think that roads and drains ought to be maintained by private enterprise and not by the State, might almost be numbered on the fingers of one hand. There is a much larger body of opinion hostile to State poor relief, but the objections commonly urged against it mostly apply with equal or greater force to the private almsgiving which would prevail in the absence of State poor relief.

The effect of the gratuitous provision of benefits by the State upon the particular welfare of individuals—on their relative wealth—though perhaps less important, is more easy to demonstrate than its effect on the general welfare. The taxpayers pay for the 'gratuitous' benefits, but all the inhabitants of a country are not taxpayers, and those who do pay taxes do not pay a large or small amount of taxation according as they receive a large or small amount of benefit. The paupers in workhouses, whose whole maintenance is provided by the State, pay nothing at all for the benefit they thus receive, except a small amount in the few cases where the work they do is worth more

§ 4. BENEFITS GRANTED BY THE STATE.

than the cost of inducing them to do it. The children for whom the State provides a gratuitous or nearly gratuitous elementary education pay nothing for that education, and their parents pay at the most only a small proportion of its cost; the fees do not amount to a large proportion of the whole cost, and the burden of school rates and of the imperial grants for education is borne by the childless as well as by those who are parents, and by those whose children are not sent to the schools maintained or subsidised by the State, as well as by those whose children do attend such schools. It is of course impossible to make paupers pay for their maintenance, and to make children pay for their schooling. It is also impossible to make each individual pay for the defence of the country in proportion to the advantage he personally receives from that defence, and it is equally impossible to make each individual pay for the police and the law courts in proportion as he has been protected in person and property from criminals and swindlers. Payments for the use of roads, sewers, and public parks can sometimes be exacted from individuals in some kind of proportion to the use they make of these things, but the proportion must necessarily be very inexact.

By distributing benefits among individuals in proportions other than those in which they contribute to its revenue the State obviously affects the relative size of individuals' incomes. What the effect actually is, of course depends on the way in which the benefits are distributed, taken together with the way in which the burden of taxation is distributed.

At the present time the ideal standard for the distribution of State benefits is generally considered by Europeans to be equality. It is supposed that every one ought, so far as possible, to derive equal advantage from the existence and action of the State. As regards some benefits this ideal of equality is actually aimed at in practice. The State endeavours to give every one equal protection from violence and fraud, equal use of many kinds of State property, such as highways and public parks, equal freedom from noxious vapours, and so on. But even in the case of these benefits the ideal is not nearly attained. Some are assaulted, robbed, defrauded, and libelled, while others escape without these injuries. Roads and drains are not equally good all over a district; nor are pleasure grounds equidistant from all men's houses. Yet the ideal of equality in the distribution of these benefits is generally striven after, and authorities receive praise or blame in proportion as they approach it more or less nearly. In the case of several benefits however, the ideal of equality is not respected in the same way. The State does not attempt to administer poor relief equally to all citizens, but only to those who need it; and to those who need it, it is administered not equally, but in proportion to their need. In the distribution of the benefit of gratuitous or nearly gratuitous State elementary education there is some pretence of maintaining equality, but it is a hollow one; the schools may be open to all children, but the children of wealthy parents are not sent to them, so that the nearly gratuitous teaching is of no advantage to the wealthy, while to the poorest class it is an enormous boon, since it helps to equalise earnings in different occupations by reducing the number of those who are so totally ignorant as to be only fit for labour which requires the smallest amount of knowledge and intelligence. Again, though everyone may, if he pleases, deposit a certain sum in the State Savings Bank, that bank is not, and is not intended to be, a benefit to the wealthy. Many minor benefits, a considerable number of which are the result of recent legislation, are distributed by the State in this country to the non-wealthy classes only.

The general rule then in this country, at all events, may be said to be that the State attempts either to distribute its benefits equally or to give greater benefits to the classes which are not rich than to those which are rich. Consequently the present distribution of State benefits tends to make incomes more equal than they would be if State benefits could be supposed not to exist. An equal addition to every one's income, however small, obviously makes incomes more equal than they would otherwise be; so, for instance, if a poor man and a rich man be given the equal enjoyment of a public park, the poor man's material welfare will be larger in proportion to the rich man's than it would be in the absence of the park. Consequently, when the State distributes benefits equally, it to some extent equalises the incomes of individuals. When it gives larger benefits to the poor than to the rich it tends to equalise incomes still more.

§ 5. CONTRIBUTIONS TO THE STATE.

Some of the benefits which the State confers on individuals it is able to confer simply in virtue of its ownership of property, by allowing individuals to use such property as roads, sewers, and pleasure grounds without payment. The rest of the benefits which the State confers must have been produced by human labour performed either voluntarily or under the laws. The abstraction called 'the State' can itself, of course, no more labour than it can enjoy.

The simplest method by which a State can command labour is to order a certain number of its subjects to do the work required. 'Forced labour' now, however, plays but a small part in the economy of European nations; the only important case in which it still subsists is the compulsory military service of the great Continental States. Such service is never really 'universal,' because many men are physically unfit for it, and half the population—women—are never made liable. But at first sight it appears as if forced

§ 5. CONTRIBUTIONS TO THE STATE. 139

labour, supposing it to be equally exacted from everyone, must be an equal deduction from everyone's material welfare. This is, however, by no means the case. It is not an equal deduction from the material welfare of those who derive income from property on the one hand and from the material welfare of those who derive their income from labour on the other hand, since those whose income is derived from property continue to draw their income while performing the forced labour or compulsory service, whereas those whose income is derived from labour cease to do so. Nor is it an equal deduction from the material welfare of those who derive a large income from labour on the one hand, and from the material welfare of those who derive a small income from labour on the other hand, since he who earns a large income by his ordinary work obviously loses more by being taken away from that work than he who earns only a small income.

Most State benefits are produced by voluntary paid labour—the labour of persons whom the State employs and pays much as if it were a private individual. In order to be able to pay for work the State must have a Revenue, and we have now to consider how the State's revenue is provided. Some small portion of a State's revenue is commonly derived from property belonging to it. If we consider the State as an association in which all have an equal share, we must look on this part of the State's revenue as an equal contribution from all its subjects, for whom the property is held in trust. It is usually but a small proportion of the State's whole revenue, and is generally much less than the amount which the State has to pay as interest on its debts. The great bulk of the expenditure of the modern State is defrayed by those contributions of its subjects which are known as Taxes. Every tax without exception affects the relative material welfare of individuals, that is to say, no tax can be imposed without altering the proportions previously existing between the material welfare of individuals, and no tax after it has once been imposed can be taken off without altering the proportions existing during the maintenance of the tax.

It is true that a tax levied from individuals in exact proportion to the size of their incomes would not affect the relative size of individuals' incomes. But no tax is levied from individuals in exact, or even nearly exact, proportion to the size of their incomes. A considerable part of our own income tax is levied from the payers not even ostensibly in proportion to the size of their income, but according to a standard which has no necessary relation to the size of their income. Much of the income obtained by individuals doing their own work or using their own property is untaxed; for instance, a man pays no tax on the income he derives from using his own furniture, so that two equally rich men will pay different amounts of income tax if the one rents a furnished and the other an unfurnished house. The tax is divided in such a way that individuals are not taxed in proportion to the size of their whole income, setting all losses against all gains; since losses incurred under one of the several heads may not be deducted from gains made under another head. Further, the tax completely ignores the kind of income which is obtained by holding property which is increasing in value. If a man invests £1,000 in some land or stock now paying 4 per cent., and each year saves and invests the income, so that the £1,000 'lies at compound interest,' he will pay a large sum in income tax in the twenty years or thereabouts in which his £1,000 will become £2,000. But if he invests his £1,000 in some land or stock which brings him in no receipts for eighteen or nineteen years, but which will rise in value to £2,000 in that time, he will pay no income tax whatever, though his income is clearly as great as in the other case. Supposing defects like these to be remedied, there still remains the fact that no income tax can possibly be levied from the very poor. To say nothing of its unpopularity, it is found in practice that the collection of an income tax from the very poor costs more than it brings in. The exemption of all incomes below a certain amount is thus inevitable; and from an income tax with exemption of all incomes below a certain size there is but a short step to the establishment of a progressive income tax, that is to say, a tax under which a large income pays not only a larger absolute amount but also a larger proportion than a small income. It has often been supposed that a progressive income tax must have the effect of 'checking accumulation'; this is a mistake. No man will be restrained from making an addition to his income by the reflection that if he makes that addition he will pay a higher rate of income tax. 'But if,' it may be objected, 'the rate of the tax were higher and higher the larger the income, in time the rate would reach 100 per cent., so that the road to the workhouse would lie through the accumulation of wealth.' The answer to this is that it is not true that the rate, though increasing with the size of the income, need ever reach 100 per cent. To prevent its ever reaching 100 per cent. is a simple question of mathematics; if it is made to increase indeed, but to increase more and more slowly the larger it gets, it need not reach 100 per cent. until the size of the income is infinite. In practice, as there are no incomes above a certain size, the question is easily solved without the aid of anything more than elementary arithmetic; there could, for instance, be no danger of the rate of the tax reaching 100 per cent. on any possible income in a progression simply constructed like this:—

				£		£
1 per cent. on incomes between	200	and	400
2	,,	,,	,,	400	,,	800
3	,,	,,	,,	800	,,	1600

§ 5. CONTRIBUTIONS TO THE STATE. 143

and so on, which would give for the highest possible incomes the following rates :—

				£		£
13 per cent.	on incomes	between		819,200	and	1,638,400
14	,,	,,	,,	1,638,400	,,	3,276,800
15	,,	,,	,,	3,276,800	,,	6,553,600
16	,,	,,	,,	6,553,600	,,	13,107,200
17	,,	,,	,,	13,107,200	,,	26,214,400

Further continuation of the scale would be scarcely necessary even in the United States. The force of the great political and moral dangers which are incurred by progressive taxation is not made greater by the invention of purely imaginary economic difficulties. In our own income tax the progressive principle is established as regards incomes between £150 and £400. When the tax is sixpence in the pound, an income of £151 (which is liable to the tax on £151 less £120, i.e. £31 only) pays 15s. 6d.—a little more than one half per cent.; from this point the percentage gradually rises until an income of £399 (which is liable to the tax on £399 less £120, i.e. £279) pays £6 19s. 6d.—almost 1¾ per cent. Above £400 there is no progression, all paying 2½ per cent.

So far as either the principle of exempting small incomes or the principle of progressivity are admitted, an income tax must obviously make individuals' available incomes more equal than they would otherwise be.

The only fundamental difference between an income tax and a property tax, that is to say, a periodical tax levied from individuals in proportion to the value of their whole property, is the obvious difference that the property tax falls only on incomes derived from the possession of property. As regards incomes derived from property alone, in some respects a property tax is more exact, in others less exact than an income tax. It is easier to tell exactly what a man's money gains in a year have been than to estimate the value of his property; here the advantage lies with the income tax. On the other hand, if the value of a man's property can be obtained, it will be a more exact index to his real income, the amount he can spend without diminishing his property, than his money gains from the possession of the property. As we have already observed, the income which a man derives from using his own property for his own direct benefit generally escapes the income tax, and so also does the income derived from holding property for some years until it rises in value. A property tax would reach both these kinds of income.

Taxes on inheritances and bequests, if levied in exact proportion to the value of the inheritance or bequest, do not affect the relative size of the incomes of those who receive inheritances and bequests, but, of course, reduce the total income of such persons compared with the total income of those who receive no bequests or inheritances. Consequently their effect even in this case is to reduce inequality of incomes. If they are not levied in simple proportion to the value of the inheritance or bequest, but are graduated or progressive, they will obviously reduce inequality of incomes still more, since they will then reduce the large inheritances and bequests more than the small ones. In either case they reduce hereditary inequalities of wealth.

Taxes on particular kinds of exchanges, such as most of those taxes levied in this country by means of stamps on binding documents, are borne by the persons who profit by these exchanges: that is to say, in many cases, by the whole community. In what proportions any particular tax on an exchange is borne by the different individuals to whom that exchange is advantageous it is generally totally impossible to say.

If a tax be imposed on certain actual articles of property already in existence, it will diminish the incomes of the owners of that property. For instance, a tax upon the land of a country diminishes the incomes of the land-owners; they have to pay the tax, and they do not receive any more rent for their land in consequence of the imposition of the tax. The tax will not make land less or more plentiful or more or less wanted than before. Similarly if a tax were now imposed on all pictures painted by Turner, it would diminish the incomes of the present owners of those pictures. But if a tax be imposed on one of those numerous kinds of commodities which are being continually worn out or used up and replaced by new ones, it will diminish the available incomes of those who use or enjoy, or wish to use or enjoy, that kind of commodity or the satisfactions ultimately resulting from its use. Tax tea and the tax will fall on those who like tea; tax beer and the tax will fall on those who like beer. The tax may be levied from the consumer or user direct or from the producers or importers of the commodity, but from whomsoever it is levied it will be eventually, though in some cases not at first, paid by the consumer or user.

Examples of taxes levied directly from the users of certain kinds of commodities are afforded by our own inhabited house duty, and taxes on male servants, carriages, armorial bearings, and dogs. Taxes of this sort must always tend to restrict the use of the commodity taxed. Tax male service and some people will prefer female service; tax pleasure horses and fewer people will keep pleasure horses; tax houses in proportion to their value and many people will crush themselves into less house room. The value of the taxed commodity must consequently fall, the owners of the existing stock will sustain a loss, and the remuneration of the producers of the taxed commodity will be reduced. This reduction will, perhaps only after a long lapse of time, perhaps immediately, perhaps even by anticipation, diminish the production of the commodity, since prosperous producers who intended to retire will retire somewhat earlier, and producers who were already in difficulties will be driven to the bankruptcy court or the workhouse, and their places will not be filled. The amount of the commodity produced will then become small enough to raise its value and the remuneration of the smaller number of producers to their old height. To put the matter shortly, the imposition of such a tax, and, which is much the same thing, the increase of such a tax, damages the owners of the existing stock of the taxed commodity and the producers of the commodity, while the remission or diminution of the tax benefits them, but after the tax has been imposed for a considerable time and remains unaltered, it is paid wholly by the users or consumers of the commodity; it is no burden upon the producers.

When the tax on a commodity is levied not from the consumer or user but from the producer, as in the case of excise duties, the remuneration of the producers will be diminished directly by the deduction of the tax from their profits. This will lead, as before, to a reduction of the amount of the commodity produced, a rise in its value, and a restoration of the old remuneration to a reduced number of producers. The tax will then be borne by the users or consumers only.

In both these cases the injury inflicted upon the producers of the commodity is not to be considered as worthy of no attention because it is 'temporary.' 'Temporary' depression is a very permanent thing to those who are crushed out of a trade by it. The abstraction called the 'trade' may recover from its depression, but the human beings do not.

The effect of a tax levied from the importer of a particular kind of commodity when the production of that kind of commodity within the country is impossible, or is subject to an equivalent excise duty, needs no separate explanation. The effect of a tax levied from the importer of a particular kind of commodity when the production of that kind of commodity within the country is possible, and is not subject to an equivalent duty, has been already sufficiently discussed.

For defraying the expenses incurred by local authorities on roads, drains, bridges, public gardens, lamps, and such like things, a tax or rate upon the immovable property in the locality is obviously the only proper tax. The public road to a house or piece of land, the public sewer, which serves it, and the public garden near it, all add to the value of the use of the property. Consequently, supposing local expenditure of the character described to be defrayed from some other source than a rate upon immovable property, the owners of such property will receive a clear gift from the State. 'But,' it may be asked, 'should the tax be levied from the owners or the occupiers of the immovable property?' The answer is that the capital cost of permanent improvements ought certainly to be levied from the owners of the property, and that the cost of maintaining such improvements, when once made, should be levied from the occupiers. As to the cost of maintaining local public works, it evidently makes little difference whether this is levied in the first instance from the owners or the occupiers; for if it is levied from the owners, they will be able to charge the occupiers more rent. Practically it is much better that the rate should be levied from the occupiers, as they are more likely to keep the works in a proper state than the owners, and we may suppose that if the rate were levied from the owners, these alone would have a voice as to its expenditure. On the other hand, it makes a great difference whether the capital cost of a permanent improvement is levied from the occupiers or from the owners. Whenever the occupiers pay the cost of a permanent improvement such as making a new street or new public park, they act in the same way as a tenant who makes structural improvements to his house. So long as he merely maintains the house in repair in accordance with his covenants he only benefits himself, but when he makes structural improvements he benefits his landlord, and has only himself to thank if his rent is raised at the end of his term or lease. In just the same way, if the occupiers as a body increase the value of the use of the property they occupy by making permanent improvements at their own expense, they will be liable to an increase of rent at the end of their terms and leases, and will thus pay at any rate a part of the expense of the improvement over again. How much they will pay will plainly depend, on the average length their leases have to run. If this is a considerable period it may pay them to make the improvement, just as it sometimes pays an individual tenant to make an improvement to his house or farm. In ordinary cases it will not pay them and the cost should be borne by the owners. At the present time in this country the capital cost of new streets and drains is largely borne by the owners of the property benefited, since local authorities will not take charge of them till they are properly made. The capital cost of improvements for which the occupiers pay in the first instance is to some extent thrown on the owners by the expedient of loans, the repayment of which is spread over a considerable period of time. In the course of thirty years, or even twenty or ten, many tenancies come to an end, and in determining the new rents the rate is taken into account as well as the improvements.

INDEX.

Agriculture, 24, 25.
Bank-notes, 37, 38.
Bequest, 101, 102.
Bronze, portability of, 34, 35.
Coin, 34.
Commodity, 29.
Co-operation, its growth, 17–21.
Credit, dispenses with a medium of exchange, 36; not itself a medium of exchange, 38.
Customs duties, 121, 148.
Debts of States, 140.
Demand and supply, 74.
Differences of earnings in different occupations, 84–99, 137.
Distribution of wealth, 64, 65.
Earnings of labour, its different names, 55, 56.
Education, general and technical, 94; paid for by the State, 94, 135–137.
Employers and employed, 47–55.
Employment, general want of, impossible, 3–6; not given by exports, 124, 125.
Exchange, results of, 27, 28; different kinds of, 29; a medium of, 30–35; facilitated by credit, 35–39.
Exchangeable things, 28.
Excise, 147.
Exports, why often exceeded by imports, 123, 124; do not 'give employment,' 124, 125.
Foreign trade, advantage of, 128, 129.
Freedom to choose an occupation, 95.
Gold, portability of, 34; importation of, 122.
Hire, 61.

Houses, taxes on, 146.
Imports and exports, 121–124.
Improvements, local, 148–150.
Incomes, sources of, 39; property a source of, 39–44; derived from labour, 44–56; derived from property, 56–64; dependent on values, 64–65; how compared, 79–82; commonly considered as consisting of coin, 80; how determined when derived from labour, 82–99; how determined when derived from property, 99–102.
Income-tax, 140–143.
Independent workman, 47.
Inheritance, 101, 102.
Interest, 62–64; rate of, 103; not uniform, 104–106; how determined, 107, 108; likely to fall, 108, 109.
Knowledge, growth of, increases the productiveness of industry, 12, 13.
Labour, necessity and object of, 3–6; ways of deriving income from, 44–56; not a commodity, 49, 50; incomes from, how determined, 82–99; forced, 138, 139.
Labourers, no separate class of, 113.
Land, certain space of, necessary for productive industry, 23, 24; tax on, 145.
Loans for local improvements, 150.
Money, 30–35; why payment is made for the use of, 43.
Occupation, advantages of each, on what dependent, 86–97.
Over-population, possible, 23–25; difficult to prove the existence of, 25.

INDEX.

Owners of property, no separate class of, 113.
Poor relief, 134, 135.
Population, 21-25.
Post Office, 129, 130, 132.
Price, 69, 70.
Private property, 26, 27; in useful material objects, 39-44.
Productiveness of industry, real criterion of a community's wealth, 11; has increased and is likely to go on increasing, 12; causes of its increase, 12-21; how affected by variations of population, 21-25.
Professions, earnings in the, 88.
Profits, 55, 56.
Progressive taxation, 142, 143.
Property, why a source of income, 39-44; ways of deriving income from, 56-64; determination of incomes derived from, 99-102; how acquired, 100-102; hereditary nature of income derived from, 102.
Property and Labour, comparative position of, 102-115; do not represent individuals, 113-115.
Property-tax, 143, 144.
Protection, 121; founded on misconceptions, 121-125; effect of, 125-126; example of, 126-129.

Rates, local, 148-150.
Rent, 60, 61.
Restrictions of production, 84.
Revenue, 139.

Salary, 55.
Saving, 16, 99.
Savings-bank, 137.
Short time, 85.
Silver, portability of, 34, 35.
Slavery, 21.
Smith, Adam, on the advantages of different occupations, 87.
Speculation, 100.

Stamp duties, 145.
State, the, character of association involved in, 116-119; future action of, in economic matters, 120; can err, 120, 121; sells commodities, 129-133; gives benefits gratuitously, 133-134; thereby somewhat equalises incomes, 134-138.
State education, a double boon, 137.
State railways, 132.
Stationary state, 13.
Supply and demand, 74.

Taxes, 140; on income, 140-143; progressive, 142, 143; on property, 143, 144; on inheritances and bequests, 144, 145; on exchanges, 145; on land, 145; on commodities, 145-150.
Temporary fluctuations, serious consequences of, 92.
Training, cost of, 94-97.

Under-population, 22, 23.
Useful material objects, why desirable, 7, 8; all instruments of production, 9; cannot be divided into natural and artificial, 10; their perishability, 10, 11; accumulation of, 14-16.

Value of a commodity, 66-69; how compared, 69-71; not dependent on amount of labour, 72-74; dependent on supply and demand, 74-79.

Wages, not advanced, 51, 52; do not include the whole of the earnings of labour, 55, 56.
Wealth, 1, 2; dependent on the productiveness of industry, 11; distribution of, 64: *see* 'Income.'
Work, a universal want of, impossible, 4-6; not the same as labour, 49, 50.

THE END.

July, 1888.

The Clarendon Press, Oxford,
LIST OF SCHOOL BOOKS,

PUBLISHED FOR THE UNIVERSITY BY

HENRY FROWDE,

AT THE OXFORD UNIVERSITY PRESS WAREHOUSE,
AMEN CORNER, LONDON.

*** *All Books are bound in Cloth, unless otherwise described.*

LATIN.

Allen. *An Elementary Latin Grammar.* By J. BARROW ALLEN, M.A. *Fifty-seventh Thousand* . . . . . Extra fcap. 8vo. 2s. 6d.

Allen. *Rudimenta Latina.* By the same Author. Extra fcap. 8vo. 2s.

Allen. *A First Latin Exercise Book.* By the same Author. *Fourth Edition.* . . . . Extra fcap. 8vo. 2s. 6d.

Allen. *A Second Latin Exercise Book.* By the same Author. Extra fcap. 8vo. 3s. 6d.

[*A Key to First and Second Latin Exercise Books : for Teachers only.*]

Jerram. *Anglice Reddenda; or, Extracts, Latin and Greek, for Unseen Translation.* By C. S. JERRAM, M.A. *Fourth Edition.* Extra fcap. 8vo. 2s. 6d.

Jerram. *Anglice Reddenda.* SECOND SERIES. By C. S. JERRAM, M.A. Extra fcap. 8vo. 3s.

Jerram. *Reddenda Minora; or, Easy Passages, Latin and Greek, for Unseen Translation.* For the use of Lower Forms. Composed and selected by C. S. JERRAM, M.A. . . . . . Extra fcap. 8vo. 1s. 6d.

Lee-Warner. *Hints and Helps for Latin Elegiacs.* Extra fcap. 8vo. 3s. 6d.

[*A Key is provided: for Teachers only.*]

Lewis and Short. *A Latin Dictionary,* founded on Andrews' Edition of Freund's Latin Dictionary. By CHARLTON T. LEWIS, Ph.D., and CHARLES SHORT, LL.D. . . . . 4to. 25s.

Nunns. *First Latin Reader.* By T. J. NUNNS, M.A. *Third Edition.* Extra fcap. 8vo. 2s.

Papillon. *A Manual of Comparative Philology* as applied to the Illustration of Greek and Latin Inflections. By T. L. PAPILLON, M.A. *Third Edition.* Crown 8vo. 6s.

Ramsay. *Exercises in Latin Prose Composition.* With Introduction, Notes, and Passages of graduated difficulty for Translation into Latin. By G. G. RAMSAY, M.A., Professor of Humanity, Glasgow. *Second Edition.* Extra fcap. 8vo. 4s. 6d.

Sargent. *Passages for Translation into Latin.* By J. Y. SARGENT, M.A. *Seventh Edition.* . . . . . Extra fcap. 8vo. 2s. 6d.

[*A Key to this Edition is provided: for Teachers only.*]

Caesar. *The Commentaries* (for Schools). With Notes and Maps. By CHARLES E. MOBERLY, M.A.
 The Gallic War. Second Edition . . . . Extra fcap. 8vo. 4s. 6d.
 The Gallic War. Books I, II. *Just ready.*
 The Civil War . . . . Extra fcap. 8vo. 3s. 6d.
 The Civil War. Book I. *Second Edition.* . . Extra fcap. 8vo. 2s.

Catulli Veronensis *Carmina Selecta*, secundum recognitionem ROBINSON ELLIS, A.M. . . . . . . Extra fcap. 8vo. 3s. 6d.

Cicero. *Selection of interesting and descriptive passages.* With Notes. By HENRY WALFORD, M.A. In three Parts. *Third Edition.*
                      Extra fcap. 8vo. 4s. 6d.
 Part I. *Anecdotes from Grecian and Roman History.* . limp, 1s. 6d.
 Part II. *Omens and Dreams; Beauties of Nature.* . . limp, 1s. 6d.
 Part III. *Rome's Rule of her Provinces.* . . . . limp, 1s. 6d.

Cicero. *De Senectute.* With Introduction and Notes. By LEONARD HUXLEY, B.A. *In one or two Parts* . . . . Extra fcap. 8vo. 2s.

Cicero. *Pro Cluentio.* With Introduction and Notes. By W. RAMSAY, M.A. Edited by G. G. RAMSAY, M.A. *Second Edition.* Extra fcap. 8vo. 3s. 6d.

Cicero. *Selected Letters* (for Schools). With Notes. By the late C. E. PRICHARD, M.A., and E. R. BERNARD, M.A. *Second Edition.*
                      Extra fcap. 8vo. 3s.

Cicero. *Select Orations* (for Schools). *First Action against Verres; Oration concerning the command of Gnaeus Pompeius; Oration on behalf of Archias; Ninth Philippic Oration.* With Introduction and Notes. By J. R. KING, M.A. *Second Edition.* . . . . Extra fcap. 8vo. 2s. 6d.

Cicero. *In Q. Caecilium Divinatio* and *In C. Verrem Actio Prima.* With Introduction and Notes. By J. R. KING, M.A.
                    Extra fcap. 8vo. limp, 1s. 6d.

Cicero. *Speeches against Catilina.* With Introduction and Notes. By E. A. UPCOTT, M.A. *In one or two Parts.* . . Extra fcap. 8vo. 2s. 6d.

Cicero. *Philippic Orations.* With Notes, &c. by J. R. KING, M.A. *Second Edition.* . . . . 8vo. 10s. 6d.

Cicero. *Select Letters.* With English Introductions, Notes, and Appendices. By ALBERT WATSON, M.A. *Third Edition.* . . . 8vo. 18s.

Cicero. *Select Letters.* Text. By the same Editor. *Second Edition.*
                    Extra fcap. 8vo. 4s.

Cornelius Nepos. With Notes. By OSCAR BROWNING, M.A. *Third Edition.* Revised by W. R. INGE, M.A. . . Extra fcap. 8vo. 3s.

Horace. With a Commentary. Volume I. *The Odes, Carmen Seculare,* and *Epodes.* By EDWARD C. WICKHAM, M.A., Head Master of Wellington College. *New Edition. In one or two Parts.* Extra fcap. 8vo. 6s.

Horace. *Selected Odes.* With Notes for the use of a Fifth Form. By E. C. WICKHAM, M.A. *In one or two Parts.* . . Extra fcap. 8vo. 2s.

Juvenal. *XIII Satires.* Edited, with Introduction, Notes, etc., by C. H. PEARSON, M.A., and H. A. STRONG, M.A. . . Crown 8vo. 6s.
 Or separately, Text and Introduction, 3s.; *Notes,* 3s. 6d.

Livy. *Selections* (for Schools). With Notes and Maps. By H. LEE-WARNER, M.A. . . . . Extra fcap. 8vo
 Part I. *The Caudine Disaster.* . . . . . limp, 1s. 6d.
 Part II. *Hannibal's Campaign in Italy.* . . . . limp, 1s. 6d.
 Part III. *The Macedonian War.* . . . . . limp, 1s. 6d.

Livy. *Book I.* With Introduction, Historical Examination, and Notes. By J. R. SEELEY M.A. *Second Edition.* . . . . . 8vo. 6s.

Livy. *Books V—VII.* With Introduction and Notes. By A. R. CLUER, B.A. *Second Edition.* Revised by P. E. MATHESON, M.A. *In one or two parts.* . . . . Extra fcap. 8vo. 5s.

Livy. *Books XXI—XXIII.* With Introduction and Notes. By M. T. TATHAM, M.A. . . . . . Extra fcap. 8vo. 4s. 6d.

Livy. *Book XXII.* With Introduction and Notes. By the same Editor. *Just ready.*

Ovid. *Selections* (for the use of Schools). With Introductions and Notes, and an Appendix on the Roman Calendar. By W. RAMSAY, M.A. Edited by G. G. RAMSAY, M.A. *Third Edition.* . Extra fcap. 8vo. 5s. 6d.

Ovid. *Tristia*, Book I. Edited by S. G. OWEN, B.A.
Extra fcap. 8vo. 3s. 6d.

Persius. *The Satires.* With Translation and Commentary by J. CONINGTON, M.A., edited by H. NETTLESHIP, M.A. *Second Edition.*
8vo. 7s. 6d.

Plautus. *Captivi.* With Introduction and Notes. By W. M. LINDSAY, M.A. *In one or two Parts.* . . . . . Extra fcap. 8vo. 2s. 6d.

Plautus. *Trinummus.* With Notes and Introductions. By C. E. FREEMAN, M.A. and A. SLOMAN, M.A. . . . . Extra fcap. 8vo. 3s.

Pliny. *Selected Letters* (for Schools). With Notes. By the late C. E. PRICHARD, M.A., and E. R. BERNARD, M.A. *New Edition. In one or two Parts.* . . . . Extra fcap. 8vo. 3s.

Sallust. *Bellum Catilinarium* and *Jugurthinum.* With Introduction and Notes, by W. W. CAPES, M.A. . . . Extra fcap. 8vo. 4s. 6d.

Tacitus. *The Annals.* Books I—IV. Edited, with Introduction and Notes for the use of Schools and Junior Students, by H. FURNEAUX, M.A.
Extra fcap. 8vo. 5s.

Tacitus. *The Annals.* Book I. By the same Editor.
Extra fcap. 8vo. *limp*, 2s.

Terence. *Adelphi.* With Notes and Introductions. By A. SLOMAN, M.A. . . . . Extra fcap. 8vo. 3s.

Terence. *Andria.* With Notes and Introductions. By C. E. FREEMAN, M.A., and A. SLOMAN, M.A. . . . . . Extra fcap. 8vo. 3s.

Terence. *Phormio.* With Notes and Introductions. By A. SLOMAN, M.A. . . . . Extra fcap. 8vo. 3s.

Tibullus and **Propertius.** Edited, with Introduction and Notes, by G. G. RAMSAY, M.A. *In one or two Parts.* . . . Extra fcap. 8vo. 6s.

Virgil. With Introduction and Notes, by T. L. PAPILLON, M.A. In Two Volumes. . . . Crown 8vo. 10s. 6d.; Text separately, 4s. 6d.

Virgil. *Bucolics.* With Introduction and Notes, by C. S. JERRAM, M.A.
In one or two Parts. Extra fcap. 8vo. 2s. 6d.

Virgil. *Aeneid I.* With Introduction and Notes, by C. S. JERRAM, M.A.
Extra fcap. 8vo. *limp*, 1s. 6d.

Virgil. *Aeneid IX.* Edited with Introduction and Notes, by A. E. HAIGH, M.A. . . . . Extra fcap 8vo. *limp* 1s. 6d. *In two Parts.* 2s.

GREEK.

Chandler. *The Elements of Greek Accentuation* (for Schools). By H. W. CHANDLER, M.A. *Second Edition.* . Extra fcap. 8vo. 2s. 6d.

Liddell and Scott. *A Greek-English Lexicon*, by HENRY GEORGE LIDDELL, D.D., and ROBERT SCOTT, D.D. *Seventh Edition.* . 4to. 36s.

Liddell and Scott. *A Greek-English Lexicon*, abridged from LIDDELL and SCOTT'S 4to. edition, chiefly for the use of Schools. *Twenty-first Edition.* Square 12mo. 7s. 6d.

Veitch. *Greek Verbs, Irregular and Defective:* their forms, meaning, and quantity; embracing all the Tenses used by Greek writers, with references to the passages in which they are found. By W. VEITCH, LL.D. *Fourth Edition.* Crown 8vo. 10s. 6d.

Wordsworth. *Graecae Grammaticae Rudimenta in usum Scholarum.* Auctore CAROLO WORDSWORTH, D.C.L. *Nineteenth Edition.* . 12mo. 4s.

Wordsworth. *A Greek Primer, for the use of beginners in that Language.* By the Right Rev. CHARLES WORDSWORTH, D.C.L., Bishop of St. Andrew's. *Seventh Edition.* . . . . Extra fcap. 8vo. 1s. 6d.

Wright. *The Golden Treasury of Ancient Greek Poetry;* being a Collection of the finest passages in the Greek Classic Poets, with Introductory Notices and Notes. By R. S. WRIGHT, M.A. . . *New edition in the Press.*

Wright and Shadwell. *A Golden Treasury of Greek Prose;* being a Collection of the finest passages in the principal Greek Prose Writers, with Introductory Notices and Notes. By R. S. WRIGHT, M.A., and J. E. L. SHADWELL, M.A. . . . . Extra fcap. 8vo. 4s. 6d.

A SERIES OF GRADUATED READERS.—

Easy Greek Reader. By EVELYN ABBOTT, M.A. *In one or two Parts.* . . . . Extra fcap. 8vo. 3s.

First Greek Reader. By W. G. RUSHBROOKE, M.L., Second Classical Master at the City of London School. *Second Edition.* Extra fcap. 8vo. 2s. 6d.

Second Greek Reader. By A. M. BELL, M.A. Extra fcap. 8vo. 3s. 6d.

Fourth Greek Reader; being *Specimens of Greek Dialects.* With Introductions and Notes. By W. W. MERRY, D.D., Rector of Lincoln College. . . . . Extra fcap. 8vo. 4s. 6d.

Fifth Greek Reader. Selections from Greek Epic and Dramatic Poetry, with Introductions and Notes. By EVELYN ABBOTT, M.A. Extra fcap. 8vo. 4s. 6d.

THE GREEK TESTAMENT.—

Evangelia Sacra Graece. . . . Fcap. 8vo. *limp*, 1s. 6d.

The Greek Testament, with the Readings adopted by the Revisers of the Authorised Version.
Fcap. 8vo. 4s. 6d.; or on writing paper, with wide margin, 15s.

Novum Testamentum Graece juxta Exemplar Millianum.
18mo. 2s. 6d.; or on writing paper, with large margin, 9s.

LIST OF SCHOOL BOOKS.

Novum Testamentum Graece. Accedunt parallela S. Scripturae loca, necnon vetus capitulorum notatio et canones Eusebii. Edidit CAROLUS LLOYD, S.T.P.R., necnon Episcopus Oxoniensis.
18mo. 3*s.* ; or on writing paper, with large margin, 10*s.* 6*d.*

A Greek Testament Primer. An Easy Grammar and Reading Book for the use of Students beginning Greek. By REV. E. MILLER, M.A.
Extra fcap. 8vo. 3*s.* 6*d.*

Outlines of Textual Criticism applied to the New Testament. By C. E. HAMMOND, M.A. *Fourth Edition.* . . Extra fcap. 8vo. 3*s.* 6*d.*

Aeschylus. *Agamemnon.* With Introduction and Notes, by ARTHUR SIDGWICK, M.A. *Third Edition. In one or two Parts.* Extra fcap. 8vo. 3*s.*

Aeschylus. *Choephoroi.* With Introduction and Notes, by the same Editor. . . . . Extra fcap. 8vo. 3*s.*

Aeschylus. *Eumenides.* With Introduction and Notes, by the same Editor. *In one or two Parts.* . . . . Extra fcap. 8vo. 3*s.*

Aeschylus. *Prometheus Bound.* With Introduction and Notes, by A. O. PRICKARD, M.A. *Second Edition.* . . . Extra fcap. 8vo. 2*s.*

Aristophanes. *The Clouds.* With Introduction and Notes, by W. W. MERRY, D.D. *Second Edition.* . . . . Extra fcap. 8vo. 2*s.*

Aristophanes. *The Acharnians.* By the same Editor. *Third Edition. In one or two Parts.* . . . . Extra fcap. 8vo. 3*s.*

Aristophanes. *The Frogs.* By the same Editor. *New Edition. In one or two Parts.* . . . . Extra fcap. 8vo. 3*s.*

Aristophanes. *The Knights.* By the same Editor. *In one or two Parts.* . . . . Extra fcap. 8vo. 3*s.*

Cebes. *Tabula.* With Introduction and Notes, by C. S. JERRAM, M.A.
Extra fcap. 8vo. 2*s.* 6*d.*

Demosthenes. *Orations against Philip.* With Introduction and Notes. By EVELYN ABBOTT, M.A., and P. E. MATHESON, M.A., Vol. I. *Philippic I and Olynthiacs I—III. In one or two Parts.* . . . Extra fcap. 8vo. 3*s.*

Euripides. *Alcestis.* By C. S. JERRAM, M.A. Extra fcap. 8vo. 2*s.* 6*d.*

Euripides. *Helena.* By the same Editor. . Extra fcap. 8vo. 3*s.*

Euripides. *Heracleidae.* By the same Editor. Extra fcap. 8vo. 3*s.*

Euripides. *Iphigenia in Tauris.* With Introduction and Notes. By the same Editor. . . . . Extra fcap. 8vo. 3*s.*

Euripides. *Medea.* With Introduction, Notes and Appendices. By C. B. HEBERDEN, M.A. *In one or two Parts.* . . Extra fcap. 8vo. 2*s.*

Herodotus. Book IX. Edited with Notes, by EVELYN ABBOTT, M.A. *In one or two Parts.* . . . . . Extra fcap. 8vo. 3*s.*

Herodotus. *Selections.* Edited, with Introduction, Notes, and a Map, by W. W. MERRY, D.D. . . . . . Extra fcap. 8vo. 2*s.* 6*d.*

Homer. *Iliad,* Books I–XII. With an Introduction, a brief Homeric Grammar, and Notes. By D. B. MONRO, M.A. Extra fcap. 8vo. 6*s.*

Homer. *Iliad,* Book I. By the same Editor. *Third Edition.*
Extra fcap. 8vo. 2*s.*

Homer. *Iliad,* Books VI and XXI. With Notes, &c. By HERBERT HAILSTONE, M.A. . . . . . . Extra fcap. 8vo. 1*s.* 6*d.* each.

Homer. *Odyssey*, Books I–XII. By W. W. MERRY, D.D. *New Edition.* In one or two Parts. . . . . Extra fcap. 8vo. 5s.

Homer. *Odyssey*, Books XIII–XXIV. By the same Editor. *Second Edition.* . . . . Extra fcap. 8vo. 5s.

Homer. *Odyssey*, Books I and II. By the same Editor.
Extra fcap. 8vo. each 1s. 6d.

Lucian. *Vera Historia.* By C. S. JERRAM, M.A. *Second Edition.*
Extra fcap. 8vo. 1s. 6d.

Plato. *The Apology.* With Introduction and Notes. By ST. GEORGE STOCK, M.A. *In one or two Parts.* . . . . Extra fcap. 8vo. 2s. 6d.

Plato. *Meno.* With Introduction and Notes. By ST. GEORGE STOCK, M.A. *In one or two Parts.* . . . . . Extra fcap. 8vo. 2s. 6d.

Sophocles. (For the use of Schools.) Edited with Introductions and English Notes by LEWIS CAMPBELL, M.A., and EVELYN ABBOTT, M.A. New and Revised Edition. 2 Vols. . . . . Extra fcap. 8vo. 10s. 6d.
Sold separately, Vol. I. Text, 4s. 6d. Vol. II. Notes, 6s.

☞ *Also in single Plays. Extra fcap. 8vo. limp,*
Oedipus Tyrannus, Philoctetes. New and Revised Edition, 2s. each.
Oedipus Coloneus, Antigone. 1s. 9d. each.
Ajax, Electra, Trachiniae. 2s. each.

Sophocles. *Oedipus Rex:* Dindorf's Text, with Notes by W. BASIL JONES, D.D., Lord Bishop of S. David's. . Extra fcap. 8vo. *limp,* 1s. 6d.

Theocritus. Edited, with Notes, by H. KYNASTON, D.D. (late SNOW). *Fourth Edition.* . . . . . Extra fcap. 8vo. 4s. 6d.

Xenophon. *Easy Selections* (for Junior Classes). With a Vocabulary, Notes, and Map. By J. S. PHILLPOTTS, B.C.L., Head Master of Bedford School, and C. S. JERRAM, M.A. *Third Edition.* . Extra fcap. 8vo. 3s. 6d.

Xenophon. *Selections* (for Schools). With Notes and Maps. By J. S. PHILLPOTTS, B.C.L. *Fourth Edition.* . . Extra fcap. 8vo. 3s. 6d.

Xenophon. *Anabasis*, Book I. With Notes and Map. By J. MARSHALL, M.A., Rector of the High School, Edinburgh. . Extra fcap. 8vo. 2s. 6d.

Xenophon. *Anabasis*, Book II. With Notes and Map. By C. S. JERRAM, M.A. . . . . Extra fcap. 8vo. 2s.

Xenophon. *Anabasis*, Book III. By J. MARSHALL, M.A.
Extra fcap. 8vo. 2s. 6d.

Xenophon. *Cyropaedia*, Book I. With Introduction and Notes. By C. BIGG, D.D. . . . . Extra fcap. 8vo. 2s.

Xenophon. *Cyropaedia*, Books IV, V. With Introduction and Notes, by C. BIGG, D.D. . . . . . . Extra fcap. 8vo. 2s. 6d.

Xenophon. *Hellenica*, Books I, II. With Introduction and Notes. By G. E. UNDERHILL, M.A. . . . . . Extra fcap. 8vo. 3s.

EARLY AND MIDDLE ENGLISH, &c.

Mayhew and Skeat. *A Concise Dictionary of Middle English.* By A. L. Mayhew, M.A., and W. W. Skeat, Litt. D. . . . Crown 8vo. 7s. 6d.

Skeat. *A Concise Etymological Dictionary of the English Language.* By W. W. Skeat, Litt. D. *Third Edition.* . . . Crown 8vo. 5s. 6d.

Tancock. *An Elementary English Grammar and Exercise Book.* By O. W. Tancock, M.A., Head Master of King Edward VI's School, Norwich. *Second Edition.* . . . . Extra fcap. 8vo. 1s. 6d.

Tancock. *An English Grammar and Reading Book,* for Lower Forms in Classical Schools. By O. W. Tancock, M.A. *Fourth Edition.*
Extra fcap. 8vo. 3s. 6d.

Skeat. *The Principles of English Etymology. First Series.* By W. W. Skeat, Litt. D. . . . . Crown 8vo. 9s.

Earle. *The Philology of the English Tongue.* By J. Earle, M.A., Professor of Anglo-Saxon. *Fourth Edition.* . . Extra fcap. 8vo. 7s. 6d.

Earle. *A Book for the Beginner in Anglo-Saxon.* By the same Author. *Third Edition.* . . . . Extra fcap. 8vo. 2s. 6d.

Sweet. *An Anglo-Saxon Primer, with Grammar, Notes, and Glossary.* By Henry Sweet, M.A. *Third Edition.* . . Extra fcap. 8vo. 2s. 6d.

Sweet. *An Anglo-Saxon Reader.* In Prose and Verse. With Grammatical Introduction, Notes, and Glossary. By the same Author. *Fourth Edition, Revised and Enlarged.* . . . . Extra fcap. 8vo. 8s. 6d.

Sweet. *A Second Anglo-Saxon Reader.* By the same Author.
Extra fcap. 8vo. 4s. 6d.

Sweet. *Anglo-Saxon Reading Primers.*
   I. *Selected Homilies of Ælfric.*   Extra fcap. 8vo. *stiff covers*, 1s. 6d.
   II. *Extracts from Alfred's Orosius.* Extra fcap. 8vo. *stiff covers*, 1s. 6d.

Sweet. *First Middle English Primer, with Grammar and Glossary.* By the same Author. . . . . Extra fcap. 8vo. 2s.

Sweet. *Second Middle English Primer.* Extracts from Chaucer, with Grammar and Glossary. By the same Author. . . Extra fcap. 8vo. 2s.

Morris and Skeat. *Specimens of Early English.* A New and Revised Edition. With Introduction, Notes, and Glossarial Index.
   Part I. From Old English Homilies to King Horn (A.D. 1150 to A.D. 1300). By R. Morris, LL.D. *Second Edition.* . . Extra fcap. 8vo. 9s.
   Part II. From Robert of Gloucester to Gower (A.D. 1298 to A.D. 1393). By R. Morris, LL.D., and W. W. Skeat, Litt. D. *Third Edition*
Extra fcap. 8vo. 7s. 6d.

Skeat. *Specimens of English Literature,* from the 'Ploughmans Crede' to the 'Shepheardes Calender' (A.D. 1394 to A.D. 1579). With Introduction, Notes, and Glossarial Index. By W. W. Skeat, Litt. D. *Fourth Edition.*
Extra fcap. 8vo. 7s. 6d.

Typical Selections from the best English Writers, with Introductory Notices. *Second Edition.* In Two Volumes. Vol. I. Latimer to Berkeley. Vol. II. Pope to Macaulay. . . Extra fcap. 8vo. 3s. 6d. each.

A SERIES OF ENGLISH CLASSICS.

Langland. *The Vision of William concerning Piers the Plowman*, by WILLIAM LANGLAND. Edited by W. W. SKEAT, Litt. D. *Fourth Edition.* Extra fcap. 8vo. 4s. 6d.

Chaucer. I. *The Prologue to the Canterbury Tales; The Knightes Tale; The Nonne Prestes Tale.* Edited by R. MORRIS, LL.D. *Fifty-first Thousand.* . . . . Extra fcap. 8vo. 2s. 6d.

Chaucer. II. *The Prioresses Tale; Sir Thopas; The Monkes Tale; The Clerkes Tale; The Squieres Tale,* &c. Edited by W. W. SKEAT, Litt. D. *Third Edition.* . . . . . . Extra fcap. 8vo. 4s. 6d.

Chaucer. III. *The Tale of the Man of Lawe; The Pardoneres Tale; The Second Nonnes Tale; The Chanouns Yemannes Tale.* By the same Editor. *New Edition, Revised.* . . . . Extra fcap. 8vo. 4s. 6d.

Gamelyn, The Tale of. Edited by W. W. SKEAT, Litt. D. Extra fcap. 8vo. *stiff covers*, 1s. 6d.

Minot. *The Poems of Laurence Minot.* Edited, with Introduction and Notes, by JOSEPH HALL, M.A. . . . Extra fcap. 8vo. 4s. 6d.

Wycliffe. *The New Testament in English,* according to the Version by JOHN WYCLIFFE, about A.D. 1380, and Revised by JOHN PURVEY, about A.D. 1388. With Introduction and Glossary by W. W. SKEAT, Litt. D. Extra fcap. 8vo. 6s.

Wycliffe. *The Books of Job, Psalms, Proverbs, Ecclesiastes, and the Song of Solomon*: according to the Wycliffite Version made by NICHOLAS DE HEREFORD, about A.D. 1381, and Revised by JOHN PURVEY, about A.D. 1388. With Introduction and Glossary by W. W. SKEAT, Litt. D. Extra fcap. 8vo. 3s. 6d.

Spenser. *The Faery Queene.* Books I and II. Edited by G. W. KITCHIN, D.D.
    Book I. *Tenth Edition.* . . . . Extra fcap. 8vo. 2s. 6d.
    Book II. *Sixth Edition.* . . . . Extra fcap. 8vo. 2s. 6d.

Hooker. *Ecclesiastical Polity,* Book I. Edited by R. W. CHURCH, M.A., Dean of St. Paul's. *Second Edition.* . . . Extra fcap. 8vo. 2s

Marlowe and Greene.—MARLOWE'S *Tragical History of Dr. Faustus,* and GREENE'S *Honourable History of Friar Bacon and Friar Bungay.* Edited by A. W. WARD, M.A. *New Edition.* . . Extra fcap. 8vo. 6s. 6d.

Marlowe. *Edward II.* Edited by O. W. TANCOCK, M.A. *Second Edition.* . . . . . Extra fcap. 8vo. *Paper covers,* 2s. *cloth,* 3s.

Shakespeare. Select Plays. Edited by W. G. CLARK, M.A., and W. ALDIS WRIGHT, M.A. . . . . . Extra fcap. 8vo. *stiff covers.*
    The Merchant of Venice. 1s.   *Macbeth.* 1s. 6d.
    Richard the Second. 1s. 6d.   *Hamlet.* 2s.

Edited by W. ALDIS WRIGHT, M.A.

The Tempest. 1s. 6d.	*Coriolanus.* 2s. 6d.
As You Like It. 1s. 6d.	*Richard the Third.* 2s. 6d.
A Midsummer Night's Dream. 1s. 6d.	*Henry the Fifth.* 2s.
Twelfth Night. 1s. 6d.	*King John.* 1s. 6d.
Julius Cæsar. 2s.	*King Lear.* 1s. 6d.

LIST OF SCHOOL BOOKS. 9

Shakespeare as a Dramatic Artist; *a popular Illustration of the Principles of Scientific Criticism.* By R. G. MOULTON, M.A. Crown 8vo. 5s.

Bacon. *Advancement of Learning.* Edited by W. ALDIS WRIGHT, M.A. *Third Edition.* . . . . . Extra fcap. 8vo. 4s. 6d.

Milton. I. *Areopagitica.* With Introduction and Notes. By JOHN W. HALES, M.A. *Third Edition.* . . . . Extra fcap. 8vo. 3s.

Milton. II. *Poems.* Edited by R. C. BROWNE, M.A. 2 vols. *Fifth Edition.* . Extra fcap. 8vo. 6s. 6d. Sold separately, Vol. I. 4s., Vol. II. 3s.
In paper covers:—
Lycidas, 3d. L'Allegro, 3d. Il Penseroso, 4d. Comus, 6d.

Milton. III. *Paradise Lost.* Book I. Edited with Notes, by H. C. BEECHING, M.A. . Extra fcap. 8vo. 1s. 6d. *In white Parchment*, 3s. 6d.

Milton. IV. *Samson Agonistes.* Edited with Introduction and Notes by JOHN CHURTON COLLINS. . . . Extra fcap. 8vo. *stiff covers*, 1s.

Clarendon. *History of the Rebellion.* Book VI. Edited with Introduction and Notes by T. ARNOLD, M.A. . . Extra fcap. 8vo. 4s. 6d.

Bunyan. *The Pilgrim's Progress, Grace Abounding, Relation of the Imprisonment of Mr. John Bunyan.* Edited by E. VENABLES, M.A.
Extra fcap. 8vo. 5s. *In white Parchment*, 6s.

Dryden. *Stanzas on the Death of Oliver Cromwell; Astræa Redux; Annus Mirabilis; Absalom and Achitophel; Religio Laici; The Hind and the Panther.* Edited by W. D. CHRISTIE, M.A. . Extra fcap. 8vo. 3s. 6d.

Locke's *Conduct of the Understanding.* Edited, with Introduction, Notes, &c. by T. FOWLER, D.D. *Second Edition.* . . Extra fcap. 8vo. 2s.

Addison. *Selections from Papers in the 'Spectator.'* With Notes. By T. ARNOLD, M.A. . Extra fcap. 8vo. 4s. 6d. *In white Parchment*, 6s.

Steele. *Selected Essays from the Tatler, Spectator, and Guardian.* By AUSTIN DOBSON. . . Extra fcap. 8vo. 5s. *In white Parchment*, 7s. 6d.

Berkeley. *Select Works of Bishop Berkeley*, with an Introduction and Notes, by A. C. FRASER, LL.D. *Third Edition.* . . Crown 8vo. 7s. 6d.

Pope. I. *Essay on Man.* Edited by MARK PATTISON, B.D. *Sixth Edition.* . . . . Extra fcap. 8vo. 1s. 6d.

Pope. II. *Satires and Epistles.* By the same Editor. *Second Edition.*
Extra fcap. 8vo. 2s.

Parnell. *The Hermit.* . . . . . *Paper covers*, 2d.

Johnson. I. *Rasselas.* Edited, with Introduction and Notes, by G. BIRKBECK HILL, D.C.L. Extra fcap. 8vo. *limp*, 2s. *In white Parchment*, 3s. 6d.

Johnson. II. *Rasselas; Lives of Dryden and Pope.* Edited by ALFRED MILNES, M.A. . . . . . Extra fcap. 8vo. 4s. 6d.
Lives of Pope and Dryden. . . . *Stiff covers*, 2s. 6d.

Johnson. III. *Life of Milton.* Edited, with Notes, etc., by C. H. FIRTH, M.A. . . . Extra fcap. 8vo. *stiff covers*, 1s 6d.; *cloth*, 2s. 6d.

Johnson. IV. *Vanity of Human Wishes.* With Notes, by E. J. PAYNE, M.A. . . . . . . *Paper covers*, 4d.

Gray. *Selected Poems.* Edited by EDMUND GOSSE.
Extra fcap. 8vo. *Stiff covers*, 1s. 6d. *In white Parchment*, 3s.

Gray. *Elegy, and Ode on Eton College.* . . *Paper covers*, 2d.

Goldsmith. *Selected Poems.* Edited, with Introduction and Notes, by AUSTIN DOBSON. . . . . Extra fcap. 8vo. 3s. 6d.
In white Parchment, 4s. 6d.

Goldsmith. *The Traveller.* Edited by G. BIRKBECK HILL, D.C.L.
Extra fcap. 8vo. *stiff covers*, 1s.
The Deserted Village. . . . *Paper covers*, 2d.

Cowper. I. *The Didactic Poems of* 1782, with Selections from the Minor Pieces, A.D. 1779-1783. Edited by H. T. GRIFFITH, B.A.
Extra fcap. 8vo. 3s.

Cowper. II. *The Task, with Tirocinium,* and Selections from the Minor Poems, A.D. 1784-1799. By the same Editor. *Second Edition.*
Extra fcap. 8vo. 3s.

Burke. I. *Thoughts on the Present Discontents; the two Speeches on America.* Edited by E. J. PAYNE, M.A. *Second Edition.*
Extra fcap. 8vo. 4s. 6d.

Burke. II. *Reflections on the French Revolution.* By the same Editor. *Second Edition.* . . . . Extra fcap. 8vo. 5s.

Burke. III. *Four Letters on the Proposals for Peace with the Regicide Directory of France.* By the same Editor. *Second Edition.*
Extra fcap. 8vo. 5s.

Keats. *Hyperion,* Book I. With Notes, by W. T. ARNOLD, B.A.
Paper covers, 4d.

Byron. *Childe Harold.* With Introduction and Notes, by H. F. TOZER, M.A. . . . . Extra fcap. 8vo. 3s. 6d. *In white Parchment,* 5s.

Scott. *Lay of the Last Minstrel.* Edited with Preface and Notes by W. MINTO, M.A. With Map.
Extra fcap. 8vo. *stiff covers,* 2s. *In Ornamental Parchment,* 3s. 6d.

Scott. *Lay of the Last Minstrel.* Introduction and Canto I, with Preface and Notes by W. MINTO, M.A. . . . *Paper covers,* 6d.

FRENCH AND ITALIAN.

Brachet. *Etymological Dictionary of the French Language*, with a Preface on the Principles of French Etymology. Translated into English by G. W. KITCHIN, D.D., Dean of Winchester. *Third Edition.*
Crown 8vo. 7s. 6d.

Brachet. *Historical Grammar of the French Language.* Translated into English by G. W. KITCHIN, D.D. *Fourth Edition.*
Extra fcap. 8vo. 3s. 6d.

Saintsbury. *Primer of French Literature.* By GEORGE SAINTSBURY, M.A. *Second Edition.* . . . . . Extra fcap. 8vo. 2s.

Saintsbury. *Short History of French Literature.* By the same Author. . . . . Crown 8vo. 10s. 6d.

Saintsbury. *Specimens of French Literature.* . . Crown 8vo. 9s.

LIST OF SCHOOL BOOKS.

Beaumarchais. *Le Barbier de Séville.* With Introduction and Notes by Austin Dobson. . . . . . . Extra fcap. 8vo. 2s. 6d.

Blouët. *L'Éloquence de la Chaire et de la Tribune Françaises.* Edited by Paul Blouët, B.A. (Univ. Gallic.) Vol. I. *French Sacred Oratory.* Extra fcap. 8vo. 2s. 6d.

Corneille. *Horace.* With Introduction and Notes by George Saintsbury, M.A. . . . . . . Extra fcap. 8vo. 2s. 6d.

Corneille. *Cinna.* With Notes, Glossary, etc. By Gustave Masson, B.A. . . . . . Extra fcap. 8vo. *stiff covers,* 1s. 6d. *cloth,* 2s.

Gautier (Théophile). *Scenes of Travel.* Selected and Edited by G. Saintsbury, M.A. . . . . . . Extra fcap. 8vo. 2s.

Masson. *Louis XIV and his Contemporaries;* as described in Extracts from the best Memoirs of the Seventeenth Century. With English Notes, Genealogical Tables, &c. By Gustave Masson, B.A. Extra fcap. 8vo. 2s. 6d.

Molière. *Les Précieuses Ridicules.* With Introduction and Notes by Andrew Lang, M.A. . . . . . . Extra fcap. 8vo. 1s. 6d.

Molière. *Les Femmes Savantes.* With Notes, Glossary, etc. By Gustave Masson, B.A. . Extra fcap. 8vo. *stiff covers,* 1s. 6d. *cloth,* 2s.

Molière. *Les Fourberies de Scapin.* } With Voltaire's Life of Molière. By
Racine. *Athalie.* } Gustave Masson, B.A.
Extra fcap. 8vo. 2s. 6d.

Molière. *Les Fourberies de Scapin.* With Voltaire's Life of Molière. By Gustave Masson, B.A. . . Extra fcap. 8vo. *stiff covers,* 1s. 6d.

Musset. *On ne badine pas avec l'Amour,* and *Fantasio.* With Introduction, Notes, etc., by Walter Herries Pollock. Extra fcap. 8vo. 2s.

NOVELETTES :—

Xavier de Maistre. *Voyage autour de ma Chambre.* }
Madame de Duras. *Ourika.* } By Gustave
Erckmann-Chatrian. *Le Vieux Tailleur.* } Masson, B.A.,
Alfred de Vigny. *La Veillée de Vincennes.* } 3rd Edition
Edmond About. *Les Jumeaux de l'Hôtel Corneille.* } Ext. fcap. 8vo.
Rodolphe Töpffer. *Mésaventures d'un Écolier.* } 2s. 6d.

Voyage autour de ma Chambre, separately, limp, 1s. 6d.

Perrault. *Popular Tales.* Edited, with an Introduction on Fairy Tales, etc., by Andrew Lang, M.A. . . . . Extra fcap. 8vo. 5s. 6d.

Quinet. *Lettres à sa Mère.* Edited by G. Saintsbury, M.A.
Extra fcap. 8vo. 2s.

Racine. *Esther.* Edited by G. Saintsbury, M.A. Extra fcap. 8vo. 2s.

Racine. *Andromaque.* } With Louis Racine's Life of his Father. By
Corneille. *Le Menteur.* } Gustave Masson, B.A.
Extra fcap. 8vo. 2s. 6d.

Regnard. . . . . *Le Joueur.* } By Gustave Masson, B.A.
Brueys and Palaprat. *Le Grondeur.* } Extra fcap. 8vo. 2s. 6d.

Sainte-Beuve. *Selections from the Causeries du Lundi.* Edited by G. SAINTSBURY, M.A. . . . . Extra fcap. 8vo. 2s.

Sévigné. *Selections from the Correspondence of* **Madame de Sévigné** and her chief Contemporaries. Intended more especially for Girls' Schools. By GUSTAVE MASSON, B.A. . . . . . . Extra fcap. 8vo. 3s.

Voltaire. *Mérope.* Edited by G. SAINTSBURY, M.A. Extra fcap. 8vo. 2s.

Dante. *Selections from the 'Inferno.'* With Introduction and Notes, by H. B. COTTERILL, B.A. . . . . . Extra fcap. 8vo. 4s. 6d.

Tasso. *La Gerusalemme Liberata.* Cantos i, ii. With Introduction and Notes, by the same Editor. . . . . Extra fcap. 8vo. 2s. 6d.

GERMAN, GOTHIC, ICELANDIC, &c.

Buchheim. *Modern German Reader.* A Graduated Collection of Extracts in Prose and Poetry from Modern German writers. Edited by C. A. BUCHHEIM, Phil. Doc.
Part I. With English Notes, a Grammatical Appendix, and a complete Vocabulary. *Fourth Edition.* . . . Extra fcap. 8vo. 2s. 6d.
Part II. With English Notes and an Index. Extra fcap. 8vo. 2s. 6d.
Part III. In preparation.

Lange. *The Germans at Home*; a Practical Introduction to German Conversation, with an Appendix containing the Essentials of German Grammar. By HERMANN LANGE. *Third Edition.* . . . . 8vo. 2s. 6d.

Lange. *The German Manual*; a German Grammar, a Reading Book, and a Handbook of German Conversation. By the same Author.
8vo. 7s. 6d.

Lange. *A Grammar of the German Language*, being a reprint of the Grammar contained in *The German Manual.* By the same Author. 8vo. 3s. 6d.

Lange. *German Composition*; a Theoretical and Practical Guide to the Art of Translating English Prose into German. By the same Author. *Second Edition* . . . . 8vo. 4s. 6d.
[*A Key in Preparation.*]

Lange. *German Spelling*: A Synopsis of the Changes which it has undergone through the Government Regulations of 1880 . *Paper cover*, 6d.

Becker's Friedrich der Grosse. With an Historical Sketch of the Rise of Prussia and of the Times of Frederick the Great. With Map. Edited by C. A. BUCHHEIM, Phil. Doc. . . . Extra fcap. 8vo. 3s. 6d.

Goethe. *Egmont.* With a Life of Goethe, etc. Edited by C. A. BUCHHEIM, Phil. Doc. *Third Edition.* . . . Extra fcap. 8vo. 3s.

Goethe. *Iphigenie auf Tauris.* A Drama. With a Critical Introduction and Notes. Edited by C. A. BUCHHEIM, Phil. Doc. *Second Edition.*
Extra fcap. 8vo. 3s.

Heine's *Harzreise.* With a Life of Heine, etc. Edited by C. A. BUCHHEIM, Phil. Doc. Extra fcap. 8vo. *stiff covers*, 1s. 6d. *cloth*, 2s. 6d.

LIST OF SCHOOL BOOKS.

Heine's *Prosa*, being Selections from his Prose Works. Edited with English Notes, etc., by C. A. Buchheim, Phil. Doc. Extra fcap. 8vo. 4s. 6d.

Lessing. *Laokoon.* With Introduction, Notes, etc. By A. Hamann, Phil. Doc., M.A. . . . . Extra fcap. 8vo. 4s. 6d.

Lessing. *Minna von Barnhelm.* A Comedy. With a Life of Lessing, Critical Analysis, Complete Commentary, etc. Edited by C. A. Buchheim, Phil. Doc. *Fifth Edition.* . . . Extra fcap. 8vo. 3s. 6d.

Lessing. *Nathan der Weise.* With English Notes, etc. Edited by C. A. Buchheim, Phil. Doc. *Second Edition.* . Extra fcap. 8vo. 4s. 6d.

Niebuhr's *Griechische Heroen-Geschichten.* Tales of Greek Heroes. Edited with English Notes and a Vocabulary, by Emma S. Buchheim. Extra fcap. 8vo. *cloth*, 2s.

Schiller's *Historische Skizzen:—Egmonts Leben und Tod,* and *Belagerung von Antwerpen.* Edited by C. A. Buchheim, Phil. Doc. *Third Edition, Revised and Enlarged, with a Map.* . Extra fcap. 8vo. 2s. 6d.

Schiller. *Wilhelm Tell.* With a Life of Schiller; an Historical and Critical Introduction, Arguments, a Complete Commentary, and Map. Edited by C. A. Buchheim, Phil. Doc. *Sixth Edition.* . Extra fcap. 8vo. 3s. 6d.

Schiller. *Wilhelm Tell.* Edited by C. A. Buchheim, Phil. Doc. *School Edition.* With Map. . . . . Extra fcap. 8vo. 2s.

Schiller. *Wilhelm Tell.* Translated into English Verse by E. Massie, M.A. . . . . Extra fcap. 8vo. 5s.

Schiller. *Die Jungfrau von Orleans.* Edited by C. A. Buchheim, Phil. Doc. [*In preparation.*]

Scherer. *A History of German Literature.* By W. Scherer. Translated from the Third German Edition by Mrs. F. Conybeare. Edited by F. Max Müller. 2 vols. . . . . . . 8vo. 21s.

Max Müller. *The German Classics from the Fourth to the Nineteenth Century.* With Biographical Notices, Translations into Modern German, and Notes, by F. Max Müller, M.A. A New edition, revised, enlarged, and adapted to Wilhelm Scherer's *History of German Literature*, by F. Lichtenstein. 2 vols. . . . . Crown 8vo. 21s.

Wright. *An Old High German Primer.* With Grammar, Notes, and Glossary. By Joseph Wright, Ph.D. . . Extra fcap. 8vo. 3s. 6d.

Wright. *A Middle High German Primer.* With Grammar, Notes, and Glossary. By Joseph Wright, Ph. D. . . Extra fcap. 8vo. 3s. 6d.

Skeat. *The Gospel of St. Mark in Gothic.* Edited by W. W. Skeat, Litt. D. . . . . Extra fcap. 8vo. 4s.

Sweet. An Icelandic Primer, with Grammar, Notes, and Glossary. By Henry Sweet, M.A. . . . . . Extra fcap. 8vo. 3s. 6d.

Vigfusson and Powell. *An Icelandic Prose Reader*, with Notes, Grammar, and Glossary. By Gudbrand Vigfusson, M.A., and F. York Powell, M.A. . . . . . . Extra fcap. 8vo. 10s. 6d.

MATHEMATICS AND PHYSICAL SCIENCE.

Aldis. *A Text Book of Algebra (with Answers to the Examples).* By W. STEADMAN ALDIS, M.A. . . . . Crown 8vo. 7s. 6d.

Hamilton and Ball. *Book-keeping.* By Sir R. G. C. HAMILTON, K.C.B., and JOHN BALL (of the firm of Quilter, Ball, & Co.). *New and Enlarged Edition* . . . . Extra fcap. 8vo. 2s.

⁂ *Ruled Exercise Books adapted to the above.* (Fcap. folio, 2s.)

Hensley. *Figures made Easy: a first Arithmetic Book.* By LEWIS HENSLEY, M.A. . . . . Crown 8vo. 6d.

Hensley. *Answers to the Examples in Figures made Easy*, together with 2000 additional Examples formed from the Tables in the same, with Answers. By the same Author. . . . . . Crown 8vo. 1s.

Hensley. *The Scholar's Arithmetic.* By the same Author.
Crown 8vo. 2s. 6d.

Hensley. *Answers to the Examples in the Scholar's Arithmetic.* By the same Author. . . . . Crown 8vo. 1s. 6d.

Hensley. *The Scholar's Algebra.* An Introductory work on Algebra. By the same Author. . . . . Crown 8vo. 2s. 6d.

Baynes. *Lessons on Thermodynamics.* By R. E. BAYNES, M.A., Lee's Reader in Physics. . . . . Crown 8vo. 7s. 6d.

Donkin. *Acoustics.* By W. F. DONKIN, M.A., F.R.S. *Second Edition.*
Crown 8vo. 7s. 6d.

Euclid Revised. Containing the essentials of the Elements of Plane Geometry as given by Euclid in his First Six Books. Edited by R. C. J. NIXON, M.A. . . . . Crown 8vo.

May likewise be had in parts as follows:—

Book I, 1s. Books I, II, 1s. 6d. Books I-IV, 3s. Books V-IV, 3s.

Euclid. *Geometry in Space.* Containing parts of Euclid's Eleventh and Twelfth Books. By the same Editor. . . . Crown 8vo. 3s. 6d.

Harcourt and Madan. *Exercises in Practical Chemistry.* Vol. I. *Elementary Exercises.* By A. G. VERNON HARCOURT, M.A.; and H. G. MADAN, M.A. *Fourth Edition.* Revised by H. G. Madan, M.A.
Crown 8vo. 10s. 6d.

Madan. *Tables of Qualitative Analysis.* Arranged by H. G. MADAN, M.A. . . . . Large 4to. 4s. 6d.

Maxwell. *An Elementary Treatise on Electricity.* By J. CLERK MAXWELL, M.A., F.R.S. Edited by W. GARNETT, M.A. Demy 8vo. 7s. 6d.

Stewart. *A Treatise on Heat*, with numerous Woodcuts and Diagrams. By BALFOUR STEWART, LL.D., F.R.S., Professor of Natural Philosophy in Owens College, Manchester. *Fifth Edition.* . Extra fcap. 8vo. 7s. 6d.

Williamson. *Chemistry for Students.* By A. W. WILLIAMSON, Phil. Doc., F.R.S., Professor of Chemistry, University College London. *A new Edition with Solutions.* . . . . . Extra fcap. 8vo. 8s. 6d.

Combination Chemical Labels. In two Parts, gummed ready for use. Part I, Basic Radicles and Names of Elements. Part II, Acid Radicles. Price 3s. 6d.

HISTORY, POLITICAL ECONOMY, GEOGRAPHY, &c.

Danson. The Wealth of Households. By J. T. DANSON. Cr. 8vo. 5s.

Freeman. *A Short History of the Norman Conquest of England.* By E. A. FREEMAN, M.A. *Second Edition.* . Extra fcap. 8vo. 2s. 6d.

George. *Genealogical Tables illustrative of Modern History.* By H. B. GEORGE, M.A. *Third Edition, Revised and Enlarged.* Small 4to. 12s.

Hughes (Alfred). *Geography for Schools.* Part I, *Practical Geography.* With Diagrams. . . . . Extra fcap. 8vo. 2s. 6d.

Kitchin. *A History of France.* With Numerous Maps, Plans, and Tables. By G. W. KITCHIN, D.D., Dean of Winchester. *Second Edition.* Vol. I. To 1453. Vol. II. 1453–1624. Vol. III. 1624–1793. each 10s. 6d.

Lucas. *Introduction to a Historical Geography of the British Colonies.* By C. P. LUCAS, B.A. . . . . Crown 8vo., with 8 maps, 4s. 6d.

Rawlinson. *A Manual of Ancient History.* By G. RAWLINSON, M.A., Camden Professor of Ancient History. *Second Edition.* Demy 8vo. 14s.

Rogers. *A Manual of Political Economy,* for the use of Schools. By J. E. THOROLD ROGERS, M.A. *Third Edition.* Extra fcap. 8vo. 4s. 6d.

Stubbs. *The Constitutional History of England, in its Origin and Development.* By WILLIAM STUBBS, D.D., Lord Bishop of Chester. Three vols. . . . . Crown 8vo. each 12s.

Stubbs. *Select Charters and other Illustrations of English Constitutional History,* from the Earliest Times to the Reign of Edward I. Arranged and edited by W. STUBBS, D.D. *Fourth Edition.* Crown 8vo. 8s. 6d.

Stubbs. *Magna Carta*: a careful reprint. . . . 4to. stitched, 1s.

ART.

Hullah. *The Cultivation of the Speaking Voice.* By JOHN HULLAH. Extra fcap. 8vo. 2s. 6d.

Maclaren. *A System of Physical Education: Theoretical and Practical.* With 346 Illustrations drawn by A. MACDONALD, of the Oxford School of Art. By ARCHIBALD MACLAREN, the Gymnasium, Oxford. *Second Edition.* Extra fcap. 8vo. 7s. 6d.

Troutbeck and Dale. *A Music Primer for Schools.* By J. TROUTBECK, D.D., formerly Music Master in Westminster School, and R. F. DALE, M.A., B. Mus., late Assistant Master in Westminster School. Crown 8vo. 1s. 6d.

Tyrwhitt. *A Handbook of Pictorial Art.* By R. St. J. TYRWHITT, M.A. With coloured Illustrations, Photographs, and a chapter on Perspective, by A. MACDONALD. *Second Edition.* . . . 8vo. *half morocco,* 18s.

Upcott. *An Introduction to Greek Sculpture.* By L. E. UPCOTT, M.A. . . . . Crown 8vo. 4s. 6d.

Student's Handbook to the University and Colleges of Oxford. *Ninth Edition.* . . . . Crown 8vo. 2s. 6d.

Helps to the Study of the Bible, taken from the *Oxford Bible for Teachers,* comprising Summaries of the several Books, with copious Explanatory Notes and Tables illustrative of Scripture History and the Characteristics of Bible Lands; with a complete Index of Subjects, a Concordance, a Dictionary of Proper Names, and a series of Maps. . . . Crown 8vo. 3s. 6d.

※ A READING ROOM *has been opened at the* CLARENDON PRESS WAREHOUSE, AMEN CORNER, *where visitors will find every facility for examining old and new works issued from the Press, and for consulting all official publications.*

☛ *All communications relating to Books included in this List, and offers of new Books and new Editions, should be addressed to*

THE SECRETARY TO THE DELEGATES,
CLARENDON PRESS,
OXFORD.

𝕷𝖔𝖓𝖉𝖔𝖓 : HENRY FROWDE,
OXFORD UNIVERSITY PRESS WAREHOUSE, AMEN CORNER.
𝕰𝖉𝖎𝖓𝖇𝖚𝖗𝖌𝖍 : 6 QUEEN STREET.
𝕺𝖝𝖋𝖔𝖗𝖉 : CLARENDON PRESS DEPOSITORY,
116 HIGH STREET.

Ec
C284el

956

Author Cannan, Edwin

Title Elementary political economy.

ELEMENTARY POLITICS

BY

THOMAS RALEIGH, M.A.

Opinions of the Press.

'One could not wish for a more impartial summary of the principles which lie at the root of all government than Mr. Raleigh has compressed into the compass of a shilling volume. There is a thorough healthy tone about this little work which ought to recommend it to all parties, except those whose doctrines and cries will not stand analysis.'—THE TIMES.

'Few books have been produced in late years better calculated to disseminate sound political knowledge and ideas.'—SCOTSMAN.

'It is difficult to imagine an elector of so low an intellectual level that he would be unable to find something in this book which he could understand; and it is almost as difficult to conceive of one of such high intellectual power and so profoundly versed in politics that he would find nothing by which he might profit.'—ST. JAMES'S GAZETTE.

'It is always desirable to remind the mass of electors that there are political principles as well as political catchwords, and also to show them that those principles have a direct bearing upon the disputed questions of the day. Mr. Raleigh has done this with great skill, and in a style which for clearness and force leaves nothing to be desired.'—DAILY NEWS.

'A healthy and timely book.. Mr. Raleigh is to be congratulated. His book only costs a shilling; but if everybody in the United Kingdom who has a vote and knows nothing about politics buys a copy Mr. Raleigh will, in the present depression of the landed interest, be able to acquire a very handsome estate.'—SATURDAY REVIEW.

'Mr. Raleigh's modest little shilling volume of 100 pp. is in every way admirable, and contains more political philosophy than any work of double its size with which we are acquainted.'—WESTMINSTER REVIEW.

'We would commend Mr. Raleigh as a competent impartial guide, and point out what a suggestive text class-book "Elementary Politics" would make to be read with a Sixth Form when explained, expanded and illustrated from ancient and modern history by a competent master.... The book as a primer of politics is perfect.' JOURNAL OF EDUCATION.

LONDON: HENRY FROWDE,

OXFORD UNIVERSITY PRESS WAREHOUSE, AMEN CORNER, E.C.

www.ingramcontent.com/pod-product-compliance
Lightning Source LLC
Chambersburg PA
CBHW031448160426
43195CB00010BB/907